Edition Centaurus – Jugend, Migration und Diversity

Herausgegeben von
K. Nowacki, Dortmund, Deutschland
A. Toprak, Dortmund, Deutschland

In der Reihe „Edition Centaurus – Jugend, Migration und Diversity" erscheinen Arbeiten, die sich mit den Belangen von Kindern und Jugendlichen, den Themen der Migration/Integration oder der Diversity im Sinne der Vielfalt befassen. Vor dem Hintergrund der These, dass wir in einer Gesellschaft kultureller Vielfalt mit verschiedenen Anliegen spezifischer Zielgruppen leben, sollen zum einen deren Besonderheiten herausgearbeitet und mögliche Unterstützungsansätze aber auch gesellschaftliche sowie politische Implikationen diskutiert werden. Insgesamt wird eine inter- bzw. transdisziplinäre Herangehensweise gewünscht. Die Reihe ist ursprünglich erschienen mit dem Titel „Gender and Diversity".

Herausgegeben von
Katja Nowacki
FH Dortmund
Dortmund, Deutschland

Ahmet Toprak
Angewandte Sozialwissenschaften
FH Dortmund
Dortmund, Deutschland

Ingrid Harrington · Nicole Kastirke
Laura Holtbrink
(Hrsg.)

Inklusion in Deutschland und Australien

Springer VS

Herausgeber
Ingrid Harrington
Inverell, New South Wales, Australien

Laura Holtbrink
Dortmund, Deutschland

Nicole Kastirke
Dortmund, Deutschland

Edition Centaurus – Jugend, Migration und Diversity
ISBN 978-3-658-14462-3   ISBN 978-3-658-14463-0 (eBook)
DOI 10.1007/978-3-658-14463-0

Die Deutsche Nationalbibliothek verzeichnet diese Publikation in der Deutschen National-
bibliografie; detaillierte bibliografische Daten sind im Internet über http://dnb.d-nb.de abrufbar.

Springer VS
© Springer Fachmedien Wiesbaden 2016
Das Werk einschließlich aller seiner Teile ist urheberrechtlich geschützt. Jede Verwertung, die
nicht ausdrücklich vom Urheberrechtsgesetz zugelassen ist, bedarf der vorherigen Zustimmung
des Verlags. Das gilt insbesondere für Vervielfältigungen, Bearbeitungen, Übersetzungen,
Mikroverfilmungen und die Einspeicherung und Verarbeitung in elektronischen Systemen.
Die Wiedergabe von Gebrauchsnamen, Handelsnamen, Warenbezeichnungen usw. in diesem
Werk berechtigt auch ohne besondere Kennzeichnung nicht zu der Annahme, dass solche
Namen im Sinne der Warenzeichen- und Markenschutz-Gesetzgebung als frei zu betrachten
wären und daher von jedermann benutzt werden dürften.
Der Verlag, die Autoren und die Herausgeber gehen davon aus, dass die Angaben und Informa-
tionen in diesem Werk zum Zeitpunkt der Veröffentlichung vollständig und korrekt sind.
Weder der Verlag noch die Autoren oder die Herausgeber übernehmen, ausdrücklich oder
implizit, Gewähr für den Inhalt des Werkes, etwaige Fehler oder Äußerungen.

Gedruckt auf säurefreiem und chlorfrei gebleichtem Papier

Springer VS ist Teil von Springer Nature
Die eingetragene Gesellschaft ist Springer Fachmedien Wiesbaden GmbH

Inhaltsverzeichnis

1   **Inklusion in Australien Was kann Deutschland von „Down Under" lernen?** 13
    1.1   Integration und Inklusion 13
    1.2   Inklusion 15
    1.3   Inklusion aus deutscher Sicht 16
    1.4   Inklusion aus australischer Sicht 17
    1.5   Umsetzung in der Ausbildung von Fachkräften 19
    1.6   Fazit 20
    1.7   Literatur 22

2   **Inclusion in Australian Public New South Wales Primary Schools: What Germany can learn from "Down Under"** 23
    2.1   Abstract 23
    2.2   Integration and Inclusion 23
    2.3   Inclusion 25
    2.4   Inclusion: German Context 25
    2.5   Inclusion: Australian Context 26
    2.6   Summary and Future Recommendations 29
    2.7   Conclusion 30
    2.8   References 30

3   **The Role of Parents, Teachers and Social Workers in the German and Australian Education Systems** 33
    3.1   Abstract 33
    3.2   Introduction 33
    3.3   Literature Review 34

3.4	The NSW Education System	34
3.5	The German Education System	39
3.6	Comparison of the German and Australian education systems	41
3.7	Methodology	42
3.7.1	Semi-structured, informal interviews	44
3.7.2	Choice of schools	46
3.8	Demographic Profiles	46
3.8.1	School A (Primary)	46
3.8.2	School B (Primary)	48
3.8.3	Primary Schools	49
3.8.4	School C (Primary)	50
3.8.5	The Secondary School D	53
3.9	Data Analysis	55
3.9.1	Participant observation	55
3.9.2	Summary	56
3.10	Discussion	56
3.10.1	The German Education System:	56
3.10.2	The NSW Education System:	59
3.10.3	Future Recommendations	61
3.11	References	63
4	**Die Rolle von Eltern, LehrerInnen und SozialarbeiterInnen im deutschen und australischen Bildungssystem**	**65**
4.1	Zusammenfassung	65
4.2	Einleitung	65
4.3	Literaturüberblick	67
4.3.1	Das Bildungssystem in NSW	67
4.3.2	Das deutsche Bildungssystem	71
4.3.3	Vergleich des deutschen und des australischen Bildungssystems	72
4.4	Methodik	74

4.4.1 Halbstrukturierte, informelle Interviews ... 75
4.4.2 Auswahl der Schulen ... 77
4.5 Demografische Profile ... 78
4.5.1 Schule A (Grundschule) ... 78
4.5.2 Schule B (Grundschule) ... 80
4.5.3 Schule C (Grundschule) ... 82
4.5.4 Vergleich ... 84
4.5.5 Weiterführende Schule D ... 85
4.5.6 Auswertung der Daten ... 87
4.5.7 Zusammenfassung ... 87
4.6 Diskussion ... 88
4.6.1 Das deutsche Bildungssystem: ... 88
4.6.2 Das Bildungssystem in NSW: ... 90
4.6.3 Empfehlungen für die Zukunft ... 92
4.7 Literatur ... 94

5 **An Exploration of how Inclusive Practices in Schools Influence Student Behaviour ... 97**
5.1 Abstract ... 97
5.2 . Literature Review ... 97
5.3 Collecting and Description of the Sample ... 99
5.3.1 Construction of the Questionnaire ... 99
5.4 Results ... 100
5.4.1 Socialisation of Students ... 100
5.4.2 Negative School Experiences ... 102
5.4.3 Problem and Conflict Resolution ... 102
5.4.4 Positive and Negative Influence by Parents and Teachers ... 102
5.4.5 Student Attitudes towards School and Free Time ... 103
5.5 Discussion ... 104
5.5.1 Social Inclusion ... 104

5.5.2	Negative Experiences	105
5.5.3	Problem and Conflict Solving	105
5.5.4	Positive or Negative Influence of Parents and Teachers	106
5.5.5	Attitude towards School and Free Time	106
5.6	Limitations of the Study	107
5.7	Conclusion	107
5.8	References:	107

6 Inklusive Schulen - Inklusive Lehrkräfte? Wie viel Sonderpädagogik braucht das Lehramtsstudium, damit Lehrkräfte auch für inklusive Schulsysteme ausgebildet sind? 109

6.1	Zusammenfassung	109
6.2	Inklusive Schulen in Deutschland und ihre Herausforderungen	109
6.3	Die Herausforderungen der Lehrkraft an inklusiven Schulen und ihre Konsequenzen	111
6.4	Das Forschungsprojekt: Lehrkräfte an inklusiven Schulen in Armidale, Australien	114
6.5	Ergebnisse des Forschungsprojektes	115
6.6	Diskussion	120
6.7	Literaturverzeichnis	123

7 Inclusive Schools - Inclusive Teachers? How much special needs preparation does a pre-service teacher need to teach successfully in an inclusive school system? 125

7.1	Abstract	125
7.2	Inclusive Schools in Germany and Their Challenges	125
7.3	The Challenges for Teachers at Inclusive Schools and their consequences	127
7.4	The Research Project: Teachers at Inclusive Schools in Armidale, Australia Research question	129
7.5	Results of the Research Project	130
7.6	Discussion	137
7.7	References	138

Prologue

The purpose of this text is to encourage Education and Social Work students to engage in critical inquiry about inclusive educational practices, and how they differ in perspective, application and understanding of their 'place' whilst working in schools in Germany and Australia. Through a number of research studies, the 'what' and 'how' inclusive practices manifest in schools are explored, in the local and the wider social/cultural contexts. The intent of the chapters is to provide both theoretical frameworks and conceptual tools to inform students' inquiry with knowledge about the debates, arguments and research findings around the educational issue of school-based inclusiveness. Critical engagement with these topics and about their implications for curriculum policies and practices can deepen and situate student inquiries in a wider context beyond personal experience and opinion. A unique feature of this book is its bilingual nature in order to increase access to both English and German speaking readers.

The text shows a broad range of perspectives including those of parents, teachers, social workers and some school executives. Central to the text is the dichotomy of perspective and practice surrounding whole-school inclusion in educational settings. Australia adopted an inclusion policy in 1999 to be applied to every government State school, based on the recommendations of the *Salamanca* Statement (1999). Essentially this shift in direction meant that all students – regardless of learning disability and/or difficulty – would be included in the educational curricula of mainstream schools. Such a shift in policy was not without its critics and difficulties, which hampered a smooth transition to an inclusive school. The main voice opposing such a shift was from teachers who claimed they lacked the specialist skills, and were not trained nor adequately prepared to successfully meet the educational and social needs of all students in their class, especially those classified as having 'special needs'. Empowerment of knowledge and strategies in classroom management were the key that ultimately saw inclusive schools in Australia become a reality.

As the global trend of inclusiveness in schools spread, so too did the challenges and the realities many traditionally run education departments faced in embracing the shift. This text explores some of the challenges the German educational department has, and continues to have, in the implementation of inclusive practices in their schools. The ramifications are huge for the whole German education system, as it means the re-classifying and assignment of students who normally would have been placed outside of the mainstream education system, into the system. The chapters interrogate the success of the Australian inclusive education policy implementation, and reflect upon what and how the German education system can learn from their experiences.

The text is the result of an on-going collaborative and productive relationship between the University of Dortmund Germany, and the University of New England, NSW Australia. The text compiles the final year Social Work students' theses in 2012, required to meet the requirements of the Bachelor of Social Work/Education at the University of Dortmund. Their work has been replicated in German by Laura Holtbrink, and Dr Ingrid Harrington has provided the English version.

In Chapters 1&2, Tonia Kasper and Ingrid Harrington take a reflective stance at the triumphs and difficulties of the Australian inclusive experience, and explore what the German system attempting the same shift could learn from their Australian neighbours.

In Chapters 2&3, Hayley Matas and Ingrid Harrington take an infantry of roles and responsibilities of the school staffing communities in both German and Australian schools. The study uncovers significant differences in the number, profession and role staff have between the two systems, and the impact upon students.

In Chapter 4, Hanna Middendorf and Ingrid Harrington explore how inclusive practices in schools impact upon the behaviour of students in the classroom. An insight into teaching pedagogy and the difficulties of student engagement, performance and retention are discussed.

In Chapters 5&6, Katharina Steinbeck and Ingrid Harrington question the amount, quality and nature of teacher preparation in order to successfully teach in an inclusive schools. An area of great debate and on-going concern, the chapter highlights characteristics and qualities best suited for teachers in inclusive classrooms.

It is anticipated that the readers of this text will be motivated to analyse and interrogate the difficult journey awaiting the challenging shift of 'exclusion' to 'inclusion' for any educational system. In doing so, readers should also be able to appreciate the great benefits and advantages to the entire school community of embracing a whole-school inclusive educational policy.

Dr Ingrid Harrington
Dr Ingrid Harrington has extensive experience working across all levels of Primary and Secondary schools in Australia. She is employed by the University of New England, Armidale, NSW Australia, as a Senior Lecturer teaching classroom and behaviour management units offered in a range of under- and post-graduate education degrees. Her research interests include improving the quality of school-based student and teacher experiences through effective classroom behaviour management strategies and techniques.

Vorwort

Der Inklusionsbegriff wird derzeit weltweit eingesetzt und in den unterschiedlichsten Facetten ausgestaltet. Eine Gruppe von Studentinnen der Sozialen Arbeit (B.A.) an der Fachhochschule Dortmund und ein australisches Team der University of New England, Armidale, Australien, haben in den Jahren 2012 und 2013 Schulen in Deutschland und Australien besucht und nach ihren Inklusionsmerkmalen untersucht. Ergebnisse dieser Studien flossen in Abschlussarbeiten ein und werden in diesem Buch in ihren zentralen Auszügen widergegeben.

Das Buch soll Studierende des Lehramtes und der Sozialen Arbeit dazu anregen, sich kritisch und forschend mit dem Phänomen der Inklusion aus einer internationalen Perspektive auseinanderzusetzen. Die einzelnen Kapitel zeigen sowohl theoretische Rahmenbedingungen als auch konzeptionelle Einblicke in das Themenfeld und untersuchen das „Was" und das „Wie" der Arbeit in Schulen vor Ort.

Ein kritischer Blick auf die Auswirkungen dieser Praktiken und Theorien auf die (bildungs-) politischen und gesellschaftlichen Entwicklungen kann diese Einblicke noch vertiefen und Studierende in ihrer Qualifikationsphase zum kritischen Reflektieren anregen. Die einzelnen Beiträge fokussieren sowohl Perspektiven der Lehrkräfte als auch der Eltern, der SchulsozialarbeiterInnen, der SchülerInnen als auch von StudentInnen in der Ausbildung.

Mit dem Schuljahr 2014/15 haben Kinder mit Behinderungen das Recht, eine Regelschule zu besuchen, in Australien wurde die sogenannte Salamanca Erklärung bereits 1999 ratifiziert.Beides hat in den jeweiligen Ländern zur Folge, dass SchülerInnen unabhängig von ihrer Behinderung oder Beeinträchtigung eine Schule besuchen dürfen, die eben nicht als „Sonderbeschulung" bezeichnet wird.

Sowohl Lehrkräfte als auch Verwaltungen sowie alle anderen Fachkräfte an Schulen waren und sind mit diesem Thema derzeit teilweise überfordert und kritisieren zu Recht die mangelnde finanzielle und personelle Ausstattung für diese Zwecke und gestalten zum Teil sehr individuelle und interessante Konzepte innerhalb von Schulen. Beispiele hierzu finden sich im Buch und sollen die Vielfalt der Ansätze deutlich machen. Die bereits längeren Erfahrungen mit dem Thema in Australien könnten Anregungen zu Vergleichen mit Deutschland liefern.

Es zeigen sich diverse Parallelen aber auch viele Unterschiede in den Zugängen zum Thema und in den praktischen Umsetzungen. Besonders manifestieren sich diese Unterschiede in dem Gebrauch der Begriffe Inklusion und Integration und der Schwierigkeit, sich in das jeweils andere Schuls- und Bildungssystem hineinzuversetzen. Die Forscherinnen haben es allerdings geschafft, sich dieser Herausforderung zu stellen und die Ausschnitte, die sie beobachten konnten, in angemessener Weise darzustellen.

In den Kapitel 1&2 reflektieren Tonia Kasper und Ingrid Harrington die Chancen und Herausforderungen der Entwicklung zur Inklusion an Schulen in Australien und versuchen herauszuarbeiten, was Deutschland von Australien lernen könnte.

In den Kapiteln 2&3 beschäftigen sich Hayley Matas und Ingrid Harrington mit den Rollen und Verantwortlichkeiten der Kollegien in deutschen und australischen Schulen. Die Studie beleuchtet die deutlichen Unterschiede innerhalb der Professionen, deren Rollen und der Rahmenbedingungen in beiden Systemen.

In Kapitel 4 untersuchen Hanna Middendorf und Ingrid Harrington, welchen Einfluss inklusive Praktiken auf das Verhalten von SchülerInnen im Klassenzimmer haben. Es wird ein Einblick in das pädagogische Handeln von Lehrkräften dessen Auswirkungen gegeben.

In den Kapiteln 5&6 fragen sich Katharina Steinbeck und Ingrid Harrington, wie die LehrerInnenausbildungen in Deutschland und Australien aufgestellt sind und ob sie sich für das Arbeiten in inklusiven Schulen eignen.

Als besonderes Merkmal dieses Buches gelten die bilingualen Texte, die allerdings keine einfachen Übersetzungen, sondern vielmehr individuelle Bearbeitungen mit Unterstützung und Beratung der jeweils deutschen oder australicshen Expertinnen sind.

Laura Holtbrink
Laura Holtbrink ist wissenschaftliche Mitarbeiterin an der Fachhochschule Dortmund. Sie arbeitet derzeitig an ihrer Dissertation zum Thema Schulsozialarbeit und Inklusion. In diesem Zusammenhang hat Sie sich intensiv mit den beiden Themen auseinandergesetzt. Dieses Wissen verbindet sie mit praktischen Erfahrungen als Schulsozialarbeiterin an einer inklusiven Grundschule.

Prof. Dr. Nicole Kastirke
Dr. Nicole Kastirke ist Professorin für Erziehungswissenschaft und Schulsozialarbeit in Dortmund und hat viele Jahre in England und in Australien an Hochschulen in der LehrerInnenausbildung mit dem Schwerpunkt Inklusion gearbeitet. Sie gibt ihre Erfahrungen heute gerne an Studierende weiter und koordiniert in regelmäßigen Abständen Exkursionen und Austausche zwischen den kooperierenden Hochschulen und ist somit gemeinsam mit ihrer australischen Kollegin, Dr. Ingrid Harrington verantwortlich für dieses Projekt.

Tonia Kasper
1 Inklusion in Australien
Was kann Deutschland von „Down Under" lernen?

Seit dem Schuljahr 2014/15 haben Kinder mit Behinderung das Recht, in einer Regelschule unterrichtet zu werden. Daher wird das Thema Inklusion in Deutschland seit einiger Zeit heftig diskutiert – vorrangig geht es dabei um die entstehenden Kosten. Das Thema hat jedoch noch andere Facetten, die es im Rahmen der Sozialen Arbeit zu beleuchten gilt. Es geht um die Frage, was Inklusion bedeutet und warum es, auch aus gesamtgesellschaftlicher Sicht, sinnvoller erscheint, diesen Begriff zu verwenden, anstatt von Integration zu sprechen.
Was verbirgt sich demnach hinter den Begrifflichkeiten Integration und Inklusion? Auf diese Frage wird im ersten Teil des Beitrages eine Antwort gegeben. Das aktuelle deutsche Inklusionskonzept steht zwar nicht im Vordergrund, wird jedoch kurz beschrieben, um es im Anschluss dem australischen Konzept gegenüberzustellen. Im Fazit wird die Leitfrage des Beitrages beantwortet.

1.1 Integration und Inklusion

Formen und Wandel von Integration

Im Folgenden werden die Begriffe „Integration" und „Inklusion" erläutert und gegeneinander abgegrenzt. Mit Hilfe der soziologischen Systemtheorie wird aufgezeigt, was Integration im Laufe der Zeit bedeutete und warum es heutzutage angemessener erscheint, von Inklusion statt von Integration zu sprechen.
Soziologisch betrachtet ist es für den Begriff der Integration wichtig zu wissen, wie innerhalb der Gesellschaft Differenzierung stattfindet, weil dadurch das Verhältnis von Gesellschaft und Individuum deutlich wird.
    Es können drei Arten von Differenzierung unterschieden werden. Die segmentäre Differenzierung ist die historisch älteste Form der Differenzierung und unterteilte die Gesellschaft in Familien, Stämme oder auch Clans, die eine in sich geschlossene Einheit bildeten. Der / Die Einzelne wurde demnach durch Geburt in seine / ihre Einheit hineingeboren und war automatisch Mitglied dieses kleinen Teils der Gesellschaft: *„Sein Integriertsein bewährte sich in der Interaktion unter Anwesenden." (Bardmann 2008, S. 53).* Die verschiedenen Einheiten oder auch

Teilsysteme waren an unterschiedlichen Orten ansässig, was gleichzeitig bedeutete, dass diese Orte die Grenzen der Gesellschaft bildeten und die Zugehörigkeit nur innerhalb dieser Grenzen galt.

Im Laufe der Zeit konnten diese Grenzen nicht mehr eingehalten werden, da einige Familien ihre Macht erweiterten - z. B. durch Handel - was zur Folge hatte, dass sich aus der segmentären Differenzierung die stratifikatorische Differenzierung herausbildete. Auch hier wurden die Menschen in ein Teilsystem hineingeboren, jedoch war die Gesellschaft nun von oben nach unten in Stände und Klassen unterteilt. Diese Form der Differenzierung war in Europa vom Spätmittelalter bis zum 17. Jahrhundert zu beobachten: *„Die Abstammung (adelig oder nicht) bestimmte die Zugehörigkeit zu einer sozialen Strata und regelte den Zugang zu den gesellschaftlichen Ressourcen."* (Bardmann 2008, S. 53).

Soziale Ungleichheiten sowie Unzulänglichkeiten brachten im Folgenden die funktionale Differenzierung hervor. Von nun an entschied nicht mehr Herkunft, sondern Leistung. Die funktionale Differenzierung ist Merkmal der modernen Gesellschaft, wobei die verschiedenen Teilsysteme unterschiedliche Funktionen erfüllen. Einige wichtige Funktionssysteme sind unter anderem: Religion, Politik, Wirtschaft, Wissenschaft, Familie sowie soziale Hilfe. Jedes dieser Teilsysteme dient der Gesellschaft auf seine Weise und ist damit exklusiv. Demnach steht nicht mehr eine Vereinheitlichung von individuellen Einstellungen im Vordergrund, sondern die Vielfalt der einzelnen Teilsysteme: *„Was die Gesellschaft zusammenhält, ist nicht der Gleichklang der individuell geglaubten und gelebten Werte, sondern das Funktionieren der Funktionskontexte – jenseits und unabhängig von individuellen Überzeugungen und Voreingenommenheiten." (Bardmann 2008, S. 54)*

Zu den intrafunktionalen Leistungsrollen der oben genannten Funktionssysteme - wie z. B. PriesterIn, PolitikerIn oder ManagerIn – gibt es in dieser Art von Differenzierung Komplementärrollen, wie hier der / die Gläubige, die WählerIn oder die ArbeitnehmerIn. In der sozialen Arbeit stehen sich SozialarbeiterIn und KlientIn gegenüber. Da die Menschen nicht mehr in ein Teilsystem hineingeboren werden, sondern „orientierungslos" zur Welt kommen, müssen sie über Leistung ihre soziale Position selbst finden: *„Die Gesellschaft muss im Gegenzug prinzipiell jedem den Zugang zu den Komplementärrollen aller ihrer Funktionssysteme eröffnen." (Bardmann 2008, S. 55)* Das bedeutet theoretisch, dass jeder Mensch in jedes Teilsystem gelangen kann, ohne Betrachtung der Herkunft bzw. individuellen Einstellung, Normen und Werte. Ob dies tatsächlich realisierbar ist, soll im Folgenden erläutert werden.

An die oben genannten Begrifflichkeiten anschließend, wird dann von Integration gesprochen, wenn verschiedene Einheiten in einem System so zusammenkommen und zusammenwirken, dass das System eine Einheit bildet und als

Einheit funktioniert, wobei ein Stabilitätsverlust und Verfall des Systems verhindert werden soll: *„Bezieht man diesen allgemeinen Integrationsbegriff auf die Integration von Menschen in soziale Zusammenhänge, so darf nach dieser Idee Integration dann als gelungen angesehen werden, wenn die Individuen so zusammenwirken, dass sie die sozialen Kontexte, letztlich die Gesellschaft als Ganze, in ihrem Bestand und in ihrem Funktionieren fördern."* (Bardmann 2008, S. 55). Integration ist demnach eine Leistung, die vom Individuum erbracht werden muss. Es gilt, gemeinsame Anschauungen, Gewohnheiten, Wertemuster und Verhaltensorientierungen zu entwickeln und nach diesen zu leben. Vermittelt werden sie z. B. durch Religion, Politik und – charakteristisch für die Moderne – durch Erziehung und Einfluss der Massenmedien: *„Individuen sind ‚integriert', wenn ihnen eben das als wichtig und richtig erscheint, was auch den anderen Individuen als wichtig und richtig erscheint, [...]."* (Bardmann 2008, S. 55). Nach dieser Ansicht wird Integration sowohl für das Individuum als auch für die Gesellschaft als erstrebenswert angesehen.

Der Gegenbegriff zu Integration ist Desintegration. Wer desintegriert ist, vermeidet gemeinsame Aktivitäten, hat kein Wir-Gefühl, leidet unter Kontrollverlust und ist in seinem individuellen Verhalten enthemmt. Desintegration wird dann zum Thema, wenn abweichendes Verhalten gehäuft zu beobachten ist oder wenn der Ruf nach einem sozialen Wandel aufkeimt. Wenn sich nichts verändern soll, erscheint Integration als ein positives Ziel, wobei sich jedoch die Frage stellt, ob es in der heutigen modernen Gesellschaft sinnvoll ist, auf Altem zu beharren statt von Neuem zu profitieren: *„Als allgemein gültig proklamierte Moralvorstellungen und Lebensmaßstäbe passen nicht zu einer freiheitlichen, individualisierten, dynamischen Lebensgestaltung, zur Pluralität der Kulturen und zur Differenziertheit der gesellschaftlichen Kontexte."* (Bardmann 2008, S. 56). Die funktional differenzierte Gesellschaft, bestehend aus verschiedenen Teilen, die ein Ganzes bilden, lebt von genau dieser Unterschiedlichkeit. Es ist fraglich, wie das Individuum sich in ein so zusammenwirkendes Ganzes überhaupt integrieren kann.

1.2 Inklusion

Aufgrund der oben ausgeführten Entwicklung hat innerhalb der Systemtheorie ein Wandel stattgefunden. Weg von der Integration, hin zu Inklusion. Hierbei geht es nicht um Ein- oder Ausschluss, sondern *„[...] Inklusion bezeichnet die Art und Weise, wie Kommunikation auf Menschen zugreift, d. h., wie die Gesellschaft, ihre Teilsysteme und deren Organisationen wie auch Interaktionen Menschen als Personen thematisieren, in Anspruch nehmen, ansprechbar machen und anschlussfähig halten."* (Bardmann 2008, S. 57). Hier lautet der Gegenbegriff Exklusion. Innerhalb dieses Schemas geht es um die Frage, inwiefern Menschen durch und mit

Kommunikation als indifferent betrachtet und dadurch als zu einem System zugehörig erachtet werden. Es geht daher nicht um den gewollten oder expliziten Ausschluss eines Individuums, sondern vielmehr darum, dass dies in der funktional differenzierten Gesellschaft durch die Verschiedenheit der Teilsysteme automatisch geschieht.Allgemein gilt in der heutigen deutschen Gesellschaft Gleichheit für alle und mögliche Teilhabe an all diesen Teilsystemen. Innerhalb der Funktionssysteme dieser Gesellschaft gibt es jedoch Voraussetzungen und Regeln, die bestimmen, wer drin und wer draußen ist: *„Die moderne Gesellschaft hat somit mit einem Selbstwiderspruch zu leben."* (Bardmann 2008, S. 59).

In diesem Beitrag steht das Funktionssystem Schule bzw. Erziehung im Vordergrund und es soll untersucht werden, ob und inwiefern hier Inklusion realisiert wird. Inklusion im schulischen Kontext bedeutet, dass kein Kind aufgrund von Beeinträchtigungen - egal welcher Art - davon ausgeschlossen werden soll bzw. darf, die bestmögliche individuelle Förderung zu bekommen: *„Ziel der Inklusion ist es, die besten Grundlagen für die Entwicklung und Ausbildung aller Kinder und Jugendlichen zu schaffen, indem Kindergärten und Schulen im Einklang mit den Ideen und Werten des Begriffs arbeiten."* (Haug 2008, S. 36). Inklusion fängt jedoch nicht erst bei tatsächlicher Präsenz jedes Kindes in einer Regelschule an, sondern beginnt schon weitaus eher: bei den politischen Rahmenbedingungen sowie der Ausstattung der Schulen und der Qualifikation der Fachkräfte. Wie dies in Deutschland und Australien umgesetzt wird, soll in den folgenden zwei Kapiteln erläutert werden.

1.3 Inklusion aus deutscher Sicht

Im deutschen Schulsystem gibt es sog. Regelschulen und Sonder- bzw. Förderschulen mit unterschiedlichen Förderschwerpunkten. Diese Schwerpunkte sind z. B. emotionale und soziale Entwicklung, geistige sowie körperliche und motorische Entwicklung oder Lernen.

Grundsätzlich haben SchülerInnen mit sonderpädagogischem Förderbedarf seit dem 9. Schulrechtsänderungsgesetz des Landes NRW, welches zum Schuljahr 2014 / 2015 in Kraft getreten ist, das Recht auf einen Platz in einer Regelschule.Für die verschiedenen Schwerpunkte gibt es entsprechende Curricula. Der Schwerpunkt emotionale und soziale Entwicklung hat eine zehnjährige Vollzeitschulpflicht, während z.B. für den Schwerpunkt geistige Entwicklung eine elfjährige Vollzeitschulpflicht besteht.

Die verschiedenen Förderschwerpunkte legen demnach von vornherein fest, dass SchülerInnen mit einem Förderbedarf bestimmten Kategorien entsprechen müssen bzw. in bestimmte Kategorien eingeteilt werden. Diesen Kategorien müssen auch die Lehrkräfte entsprechen, denn wer an einer Förderschule unterrichten möchte, muss den Studiengang Sonderpädagogik erfolgreich absolviert haben. Die zu studierenden Fächer sind - hier zum Beispiel an der Technischen Universität Dortmund - Bildungswissenschaften, zwei sonderpädagogische Schwerpunkte sowie zwei Unterrichtsfächer. Daneben werden noch die Teilbereiche Diagnose und Individuelle Förderung und Deutsch für Schülerinnen und Schüler mit Zuwanderungsgeschichte belegt. Je nach Förderschwerpunkt sind Organisation des Unterrichts und Inhalt des Unterrichts verschieden und haben unterschiedliche Bildungsabschlüsse zum Ziel.

LehrerInnen an Regelschulen müssen zwar neben ihren gewählten Fächerkombinationen auch Erziehungswissenschaften wählen, jedoch keinen sonderpädagogischen Förderbedarfsschwerpunkt. Daraus folgt, dass sich vor Beginn des Studiums für eine der beiden Möglichkeiten entschieden werden muss. Weiter bedeutet dies, dass LehrerInnen nur für ihre Zielgruppe entsprechend ausgebildet werden (Bildungsministerium des Landes NRW, 2013-2014 sowie Technische Universität Dortmund, 2014).

Genau hier liegt jedoch, neben vielen anderen Dingen, eine große Schwierigkeit, wenn SchülerInnen mit und ohne Förderbedarf gemeinsam unterrichtet werden sollen. Herausforderungen und Problematiken, die mit der Gesetzesänderung einhergehen, werden im letzten Kapitel erläutert.

1.4 Inklusion aus australischer Sicht

Umsetzung im Schulsystem
Inklusion beginnt in Australien bereits auf der sprachlichen Ebene. Wird in Deutschland von „Menschen mit Behinderung" gesprochen, heißt es in Australien „Kinder mit speziellen Bedürfnissen" („children with special needs"). Es findet demnach keine Zuschreibung statt, die explizit auf etwas hinweist, sondern es wird vor Augen geführt, dass diesen speziellen Bedürfnissen entsprochen werden muss. Nicht das Kind wird in die Pflicht genommen, sondern die Fachkräfte, die das Kind betreuen. „Special needs" sind nicht nur körperliche oder geistige Behinderungen, sondern beziehen sich auch auf Kinder, deren Eltern eine Behinderung haben; Kinder, die aus Familien der Ureinwohner Australiens stammen sowie Kinder mit kulturell unterschiedlichem Hintergrund.

Neben Regelschulen gibt es in Australien auch Schulen außerhalb des Regelsystems, die jedoch nur von einem vergleichsweise geringen Teil der Kinder besucht werden: „Es handelt sich hierbei meist um Kinder mit multipler und schwerer Behinderung." (Sens 2008, S. 285). Im Großteil der Fälle können die Eltern einen Platz in einer Regelschule einklagen – und sind damit erfolgreich, denn Regelschulen sind dazu in der Lage, nahezu alle „special needs" abzudecken.

Gleichzeitig wird den Eltern die Möglichkeit gegeben, ihre Kinder eine Sondereinrichtung besuchen zu lassen: „Das australische Bildungssystem betont somit auf der einen Seite konsequent den Inklusionsgedanken und auf der anderen Seite die Wahlfreiheit der Eltern. Dies ist eine Besonderheit des australischen Bildungssystems." (Sens 2008, S. 286).

Geht es um die Einschätzung der „special needs", wird in Australien eine Kategorisierung vermieden. Nicht jedes Kind mit Zuwanderungsgeschichte benötigt dieselbe Unterstützung. Das Kind wird individuell in seinem Kontext betrachtet und so werden die Bedürfnisse analysiert. Wichtig sind daher auch die Fachkräfte und deren Ausbildung und daraus resultierend, der Blickwinkel, aus dem auf Kinder mit „special needs" geschaut wird: „Voraussetzung hierfür ist die Schaffung einer Wissensbasis für Fachkräfte bezüglich Informationen über verschiedene Arten von Lernausgangslagen (z. B. Zweitspracherwerb), neuester empirischer Befunde der Lernforschung, struktureller und finanzieller Hilfen sowie einer gelungenen Zusammenarbeit mit den Eltern und anderen Beteiligten." (Sens 2008, S. 286). Daneben ist es in Australien üblich, dass Fachkräfte sich gut mit den kindlichen Entwicklungsphasen auskennen. Es geht demnach nicht nur um optimales Lernen, sondern auch um optimales Lehren. Dass die Individualität des Kindes im Vordergrund steht, wird daran deutlich, dass auch hochbegabte Kinder nach dem sog. nicht kategorialen Ansatz eingeschätzt werden. Daneben existieren z. B. im australischen Grundschulsystem keine verbindlichen Curricula, jeder Lehrplan ist individuell und orientiert sich am Lernprozess des Kindes.

Wird nun ein Hilfebedarf festgestellt, folgt ein individuell auf das Kind zugeschnittenes Förderprogramm. Als Beispiel dient hier das Sprachförderkonzept LOTE („Language other than English"). Kinder, die eine andere Muttersprache haben als Englisch, werden in eben dieser Muttersprache unterrichtet. Als Inhalte werden Themen aus anderen Bildungsbereichen kombiniert. Kinder, deren Muttersprache wiederum Englisch ist, lernen in diesem Unterricht gleichzeitig eine Fremdsprache: „Kinder mit besonderen Bedürfnissen erfahren somit eine Wertschätzung ihrer (sprachlichen) Kompetenzen, während zunächst monolinguale Kinder von muttersprachlichen Sprechern beim Fremdsprachenlernen profitieren." (Sens 2008, S. 288). Anders als in Deutschland wird der Fokus nicht auf die mangelnde Kenntnis der Landessprache gelegt, sondern darauf, Mehrsprachigkeit als wertvolle Ressource im Miteinander zu betrachten. Hier zeigt sich - wie einleitend erläutert – dass es nicht darum geht, eine „Behinderung" vor der Tür abzulegen, sondern darum, die speziellen Bedürfnisse von Kindern zu erkennen und sie entsprechend zu fördern.

1.5 Umsetzung in der Ausbildung von Fachkräften

Im Folgenden soll ein Blick auf die Fachkräfte bzw. deren Ausbildung geworfen werden. Es geht vor allem um den Bereich „Early Childhood", der in Australien die Lebensphase von 0 bis 8 Jahren umfasst.

Nach vier Jahren Studium mit einem B.A.-Abschluss können ErzieherInnen sowohl in einer Kindertagesstätte und in einer Grundschule ihren Beruf ausüben. Das Besondere hieran ist, dass der Wechsel zur Grundschule übergreifend gestaltet wird. GrundschullehrerInnen können sich zu ErzieherInnen weiterbilden lassen: „Der Übergang vom Elementar- in den Primarbereich gestaltet sich fließender, da auch klassisch elementarpädagogische Konzepte in den ersten beiden Schuljahren Berücksichtigung finden." (Sens 2008, S. 290). Dies trägt aber auch umgekehrt Rechnung, da LehrerInnen ihre didaktischen Grundkenntnisse in den Elementarbereich einbringen.

Nach dem Bachelor können sich AbsolventInnen weiter qualifizieren, bis zum Master und zur Promotion. Dieser Weg ist eher forschungsorientiert, wobei die AbsolventInnen hier besonders von ihrer praktischen Erfahrung profitieren: „In jedem australischen Bundesland gibt es mittlerweile einen Professor oder eine Professorin für ‚Early Childhood', die diese wissenschaftliche Position aus der Praxis erreicht haben." (Sens 2008, S. 290).

Nach Abschluss des B.A. Studiums „Early childhood and primary" (Beispiel University of New England, Armidale), zeichnen sich AbsolventInnen durch folgende Qualitätsmarkmale aus: Knowledge of Discipline („Kenntnisse des Lehrfachs"), Communication Skills („Kommunikationsfertigkeiten"), Global Perspectives („globaler Blickwinkel"), Information Literacy („Informationskompetenz"), Life-Long Learning (lebenslanges Lernen), Problem Solving (Problemlösefähigkeit), Social Responsibility (soziale Verantwortung) und Team-Work (vgl. University of New England, 2013).

Während des B.A. Studiums durchlaufen die angehenden Fachkräfte 32 Kurseinheiten, die u. a. folgende Inhalte aufweisen: Perspectives of Children and Childhood (Blickwinkel von Kindheit und Kindern), Young Children's Resilience (Belastbarkeit von jungen Kindern), Early Education Leadership Theory and Practice (Theorie und Praxis des Führungsverhaltens im Bereich der frühkindlichen Bildung), Social Justice in Early Childhood Education (Soziale Gerechtigkeit in der frühkindlichen Bildung), Literacy in Early Childhood (Lese und Schreibfähigkeit in der frühen Kindheit) sowie Inclusive and Special Education (Inklusive Pädagogik und Pädagogik für spezielle Bedürfnisse). Daneben gibt es diverse Praxiseinheiten, wie z. B. Pedagogy of Play (Spielpädagogik), Aboriginal Education („"),Planning for Effective Learning (Planung für effektives Lernen), Classroom Behaviour Management (Verhalten im Klassenraum), Introduction to Professional

Practice (Einführung in die professionelle Praxis). An dieser Ausbildung kann abgelesen werden, dass es nicht darum geht, in Methodik und Didaktik geschult zu werden, sondern dass darüber hinaus viel Wert auf Fachwissen und Hintergründe aus dem Bereich der frühen Kindheit bzw. frühkindlicher Bildung gelegt wird (vgl. University of New England, 2013).

Es kann festgehalten werden: Inklusion in Australien scheint zu funktionieren, weil nicht nur jedes Kind individuell gesehen und gefördert wird, sondern auch, weil die Ausbildung der Fachkräfte so angelegt ist, dass sie theoretisch und praktisch qualifiziert und persönlich reflektiert ins Berufsleben starten.

1.6 Fazit

Der Vergleich der Inklusionskonzepte Deutschlands und Australiens macht deutlich, dass die Einstellungen und Haltungen der im Schulsystem Tätigen Grundlage für alles Handeln sein müssen. Die Haltung beginnt im Kopf und manifestiert sich daher auch in der Ausdrucksweise. Anstatt die Wendung „Menschen mit Behinderung" zu benutzen, sollte im deutschen Sprachgebrauch nach Australien geschaut und die Wendung „Kinder mit speziellen Bedürfnissen" übernommen werden. Obwohl dies einen längeren Atem erfordert, erscheint es unverständlich, dies als Begründung heranzuziehen, die Sprache hier hingehend nicht anzupassen. In Bezug auf die Schulform wird heute von Förderschulen gesprochen und nicht mehr von Sonderschulen, jedoch nennt sich der entsprechende Studiengang immer noch Sonderpädagogik, was unglücklich gewählt ist. „Sonder" steckt im Wort sonderbar und könnte eine negative Assoziation entstehen lassen. Förderbedarf bzw. Förderung ist eher positiv belegt und bedeutet, dass Unterstützung nötig ist. Mit der Änderung im Sprachgebrauch könnte demnach ein erster kleiner Schritt getan werden. Vielleicht führt dieser weg von der unsäglichen Beschimpfung „Bist du behindert?!" auf deutschen Schulhöfen.

Bezogen auf die öffentliche Diskussion scheint es, als ginge es immer noch um die Frage, ob Inklusion in Deutschland überhaupt möglich gemacht werden soll. Mit dem Inkrafttreten der UN-Behindertenrechtskonvention im Jahr 2009 hat sich Deutschland jedoch dazu verpflichtet, Bedingungen zu schaffen, um Inklusion zu ermöglichen. Es geht also längst nicht mehr um das ob, sondern um das wie. Und das wie sieht folgendermaßen aus:

Ab dem Schuljahr 2014 / 2015 können Eltern, die ein Kind mit Förderbedarf haben, dieses Kind an einer Regelschule anmelden. Was dann folgt ist jedoch unklar geregelt: „Jedes Kind hat einen Anspruch auf Aufnahme in die seiner Wohnung nächstgelegene Grundschule der gewünschten Schulart in seiner Gemeinde im Rahmen der vom Schulträger festgelegten Aufnahmekapazität, soweit der Schulträger keinen Schuleinzugsbereich für diese Schulart gebildet hat (§ 46

Absatz 3 SchulG)." (Bildungsministerium des Landes NRW, 2013-2014). Der Schulträger kann demnach individuell eine Aufnahmekapazität festlegen und ist diese erschöpft, müssen sich die Eltern eine andere Schule aussuchen. Ist auch hier die Aufnahmekapazität erschöpft, muss weiter gesucht werden. Lässt sich keine Regelschule finden, bleibt den Eltern nichts anderes übrig, als ihr Kind doch auf einer Förderschule anzumelden, denn diese sollen, wenn sie bestimmten Kriterien wie MindestschülerInnenanzahl usw. entsprechen, weiter bestehen bleiben (vgl. Bildungsministerium des Landes NRW, 2013-2014).

Daneben gibt es viele weitere Einstellungen und Konzepte, die es wert sind, einen Blick nach Australien zu werfen. Nicht alle Kinder mit einem kulturell unterschiedlichen Hintergrund brauchen spezielle Förderung, allerdings wird der Besonderheit ihrer Zweisprachigkeit im deutschen Schulsystem nicht unmittelbar Rechnung getragen. Kinder, deren Muttersprache nicht Deutsch ist, werden bis zum entsprechenden Alter in einer Förderklasse auf einer Hauptschule gemeinsam unterrichtet, ohne nach Alter oder bisherigem Bildungsweg zu differenzieren. So kann es passieren, dass ein Kind, welches noch alphabetisiert werden muss neben einem Kind sitzt, das entsprechend seinem Leistungsniveau in die reguläre Klassenstufe gehen könnte, aber leider noch nicht ausreichend Deutsch spricht, um dies unter Beweis stellen zu können. Würde Deutschland das LOTE - Programm übernehmen, könnten auch hier die Kinder voneinander lernen und zwar gleichzeitig Sprache, Kultur sowie Unterrichtsinhalte. So könnten vielen Vorurteilen und Diskriminierungen Einhalt geboten werden.

Neben der Erweiterung des Fokus auf die Kinder muss dringend etwas an der Ausbildung von Fachkräften verbessert werden, was in Australien bereits in guten Asätzen gezeigt wird. Die ganzheitliche Betrachtung eines Kindes ist leider nicht selbstverständlich, was daran zu erkennen ist, dass sie entsprechend ihres Förderschwerpunktes in Kategorien eingeteilt werden. Mit ganzheitlich ist die Einbeziehung des persönlichen und kulturellen Hintergrundes sowie besonderen Förderbedarfes gemeint. Denn selbst ohne festgestellten Förderbedarf ist nicht längst jedes Kind in der Lage, den Schulalltag zu bewältigen. Um hier Unterstützung zu gewährleisten, gibt es an vielen Schulen SchulsozialarbeiterInnen, die allerdings häufig mit befristetetn Verträgen eingestellt werden, was eine effektive Kooperation mit den KollegInnen aus der Regel – und Sonderpädagogik schwierig macht. Da LehrerInnen für Regelschulen keine sonderpädagogische Ausbildung haben, stellt sich auch hier die Frage: Wie sieht Inklusion ab dem kommenden Schuljahr reell aus? Zwar bekommen die entsprechenden Klassen dann eine SonderpädagogIn oder Integrationshilfe gestellt, doch stehen diese häufig nicht jeder Klasse zur Verfügung. Konkrete und verbindliche Aussagen werden hier selten gegeben, doch vielleicht müssen all diese Probleme bzw. Herausforderungen gemeinsam auflaufen, damit die Politik versteht, dass ein Wandel in der Gesellschaft und im Schulsystem überfällig ist.

Damit gemeint ist, dass ein Ziel bekannt ist und erreichbar gemacht werden soll, aber nicht die entsprechenden Weichen gestellt werden – angefangen bei Rampen bzw. Fahrstühlen für RollstuhlfahrerInnen bis hin zur Umsetzung im gemeinsamen Unterricht. Häufig wird in der Presse über vermeintlich hohe Kosten für die Umsetzung von Inklusion berichtet. Dem gegenüberstellt wird die Frage der Einstellung zum Thema. Doch wären die Kosten so ein großes Thema, wenn die Einstellung stimmte? In Deutschland wird im europäischen Vergleich wenig für Bildung ausgegeben. Sind es in Australien 5,6% des BIP und in Deutschland nur 4,4% (vgl. Statista, 2012). Selbst ohne Einbeziehung von Inklusion, deren Umsetzung und den entstehenden Kosten scheint der Stellenwert von Bildung in Deutschland nicht der Höchste zu sein. Bevor also ein gesellschaftlicher Konsens zum Thema gemeinsamer Unterricht für Kinder mit und ohne Förderbedarf gefunden wird, muss vielleicht generell die Einstellung zum Thema Bildung und Chancengerechtigkeit in Deutschland unter die Lupe genommen werden.

1.7 Literatur

Bardmann, T. M. (2008). Integration und Inklusion - systemtheoretisch buchstabiert: Neue Herausforderungen für die soziale und pädagogische Arbeit. In: Ytterhus, Borgunn / Kreuzer, Max: „Dabeisein ist nicht alles." Inklusion und Zusammenleben im Kindergarten, München: Reinhardt, S. 53-70.
Haug, P. (2008). Inklusion als Herausforderung der Politik im internationalen Kontext. In: Ytterhus, Borgunn / Kreuzer, Max: „Dabeisein ist nicht alles." Inklusion und Zusammenleben im Kindergarten, München: Reinhardt, S. 36-49.
Sens, A. (2008). Inklusion im Elementarbereich und Konzepte der Ausbildung – Entwicklungen in Australien. In: Ytterhus, Borgunn / Kreuzer, Max: „Dabeisein ist nicht alles." Inklusion und Zusammenleben im Kindergarten, München: Reinhardt, S. 283-297.
Schulministerium des Landes NRW (2013-2014), Bildungsportal, http://www.schulministerium.nrw.de/docs/Schulsystem/Schulformen/Foerderschule/Foerderschwerpunkte/index.html Zugegriffen 19.02.2014
Schulministerium des Landes NRW (2013-2014), Bildungsportal,http://www.schulministerium.nrw.de/docs/Schulsystem/Inklusion/FAQ/index.html Zugegriffen 19.02.2014
http://www.schulministerium.nrw.de/docs/Schulsystem/Inklusion/FAQ/FAQ-Konvention/index.html Zugegriffen 19.02.2014
http://www.schulministerium.nrw.de/docs/Schulsystem/Inklusion/FAQ/FAQ-Konvention/index.html Zugegriffen 19.02.2014
Statista, 2014, online verfügbar
http://de.statista.com/statistik/daten/studie/150660/umfrage/oeffentliche-gesamtausgaben-fuer-bildung---top-10-nach-eu-staat/ Zugegriffen 27.05.2014
Technische Universität Dortmund, 2014, http://www.dokoll.tu-dortmund.de/cms/labg2009/de/bachelor/sp/index.html (zuletzt abgerufen am 15.06.2014)
http://www.dokoll.tu-dortmund.de/cms/labg2009/de/bachelor/sp/studienaufbau/index.html Zugegriffen 15.06.2014
University of New England, 2013, https://my.une.edu.au/courses/2014/courses/BEDECP/program-of-study.html Zugegriffen 02.06.2014
https://my.une.edu.au/courses/2014/courses/BEDECP Zugegriffen 02.06.2014

Tonia Kasper and Ingrid Harrington
2 Inclusion in Australian Public New South Wales Primary Schools: What Germany can learn from "Down Under"

2.1 Abstract

As of 2013, children with disabilities will have the right to be taught in mainstream schools. The topic of inclusion has been intensely discussed in Germany mainly with the focus on the costs that educating those with disabilities external to or within mainstream schools might rise. As German schools have social workers based in schools, the topic of inclusive educational practices in schools raises many different aspects that will be examined from a social work perspective in order to fully understand these aspects. The question of what 'inclusion' means in German schools, and why it is more appropriate to speak in terms of 'inclusion' in schools rather than 'integration' will be explored. It is important to note that whilst the current German concept of inclusion is not the main focus of this chapter, it will be briefly discussed and contrasted later with the Australian concept. Future recommendations on how to improve the current German system will be provided to at the end of the chapter.

2.2 Integration and Inclusion

Forms and Changes of Integration

The use of the terms "Integration" and "Inclusion" from a sociological perspective reinforce why it is more appropriate to use the term "inclusion" instead of "integration". The use of the term "integration" from a sociological perspective recognises and appreciates how differentiations develop in a society as it highlights the relation between a society and the individual.
   There are three distinguishable types of differentiation: i) Segmentary, ii) Stratificatory' and iii) Functional. Segmentary differentiation historically is the oldest form of differentiation and divides society into families, tribes or clans, which comprise a closed unit. Thus, an individual is born into their unit automatically becomes a member of their small part of society: "Their integration was proven by their interaction with others." (Bardmann 2008, S. 53). The different units

or subsystems residing at different locations meant that these locations flagged the borders and affiliations of society. Over time however, these borders could not be sustained because of the impact of some families' influences e.g. through trading. Consequently the Segmentary differentiation became stratified, or known today as 'Stratificatory differentiation'. In 'Statificatory' differentiation, people were also born into a subsystem, but society was divided vertically into ranks and classes. This form of differentiation can also be seen in Europe from the Late Middle Ages to the 17th century: "The ancestry (noble or not) defined the belonging to a social stratum and regulated the access to social resources." (Bardmann 2008, S. 53) Social inequalities and deficiencies lead to the third form of differentiation known as 'Functional differentiation'. It was not one's ancestry that decided their place in society, but their attainment within each functional system. In every functional system there are sets of complementary roles e.g. Priest and Believer; Politician and Voter; Employer and Employee. In the field of social work, the social worker and client form a complementary role. As people are no longer born into subsystems, but are born "un-oriented", they need to find their social position through attainment: "In return, society has to make the complementary roles of all functional systems accessible for everyone" (Bardmann 2008, S. 55). Theoretically this means that everybody can gain membership into every subsystem without looking at the ancestry, individual attitudes, norms and values.

Societal functional differentiation is a characteristic of modern society, and the three different subsystems fulfil different functions. Among others, important Functional differentiation systems include: Religious, Political, Economic, Science, Family, and Social Support. Every subsystem serves the society in its own ways, and is therefore exclusive. Thus, the standardisation of individual attitudes is no longer in the foreground, but the diversity of the subsystems: "What holds the society together is not the unison of individually lived values but the functioning of the functional context – beyond and independent from individual beliefs and biases." (Bardmann 2008, S. 54)

For the purpose of this chapter, the term 'integration' will be used when different units of a system work together so well that the system works as one unit. In doing so, a loss of stability and decay of the system is prevented: "If one applies this general definition of integration to the integration of people in a social context, so can integration be seen as successful when the individuals come together in such a way that they boost the existence and the functioning of social contexts, and finally society as a whole." (Bardmann 2008, S. 55).

Integration is an achievement that the individual has to make happen. It is thereby imperative to develop collective opinions, habits, value patterns and behavioural orientations. These are typically conveyed through religion, politics, education and mass media: "Individuals are 'integrated' when they regard the same things as important and right as other individuals […]" (Bardmann 2008, S.

55) According to this view, integration is desirable for the individual as well as for society.The counter term to 'integration' is 'disintegration'. Someone who is 'disintegrated' avoids collective activities; has no feeling of belonging to society; experiences a loss of control, and is disinhibited in their individual behaviour. Disintegration occurs when a social change is needed. If nothing needs to change, integration seems like a positive goal.

2.3 Inclusion

Based on Systems theory, there was a shift away from 'integration' towards 'inclusion': " […] Inclusion refers to how communication accesses people, that is to say how society, its subsystems and their organisations as well as interaction broach the topic of people as human beings […]" (Badmann 2008, S. 55). Here, the counter term for 'inclusion' is 'exclusion'. Typically in the modern German society of today, everybody is equal and has the possibility of partaking in every subsystem. However, within the functional systems of this society, there are conditions and rules that decide who is included and who is excluded: "Hence, the modern society has to live with a self-contradiction." (Bardmann 2008, S. 55).
This chapter will focus on the functional system of school and education from a social worker's perspective. It will examine how and in which ways inclusion is realised. Inclusion within a school context means that no child is excluded from individual support on the grounds of any impairment: "The goal of inclusion is to create the best basis for the development and education of all children and adolescents by having kinder gardens and schools work in keeping with the ideas and values of inclusion." (Haug 2008, S. 36). However, inclusion does not begin with how every child presents at a regular school, but features much earlier within the current political framework, the amount of school resources, and teacher qualifications. How these are implemented in Germany and Australia will be explained in the following two chapters.

2.4 Inclusion: German Context

The German school system has 'regular' and 'special' schools that focus on the different types and levels of student support. The different foci include emotional and social development, mental development, physical and motor development or learning. The ratification of the UN Convention on the Rights of Persons with Disabilities in 2009, flagged a change in the North Rhine-Westphalia school law to come to effect in the 2014/2015 school year, What this change means is that pupils with special educational needs, will have the right to be educated at a 'regular' school.

For different student foci, there are different curricula and requirements. By way of illustration, a student whose focus is on emotional and social development, must complete a 10-year compulsory full-time education, whereas a student focus on mental development, must complete a compulsory full-time education of 11 years. Hence, the different foci categorises from the outset which category the students with special needs belong to. The teachers have to comply with these categories because those teachers wanting to teach at a special school, need to be trained in special needs education where the subjects of study include pedagogy, two special needs foci, and two teaching subjects. At the University of Cologne, students wishing to teach in a special school need to undertake the mandatory study of the special needs focus learning subject, and the teaching subjects of Mathematics and German.

Teachers at regular schools need to choose the pedagogy subjects alongside their two chosen teaching subjects, but not necessarily a unit with a special needs education focus. This means that students choosing a teaching career decide before their teacher education begins, whether to study in a regular or special school. The ramifications of where teachers study is that they are context trained for only one of their target pupils (vgl. Bildungsministerium des Landes NRW, 2013-2014, Technische Universität Dortmund, 2014). The ramifications of such a stratified education training system becomes evident when the shift towards including all students into regular schools next year becomes a reality. Currently, children with special needs are allocated to special schools, and there is the model of joint lessons: *"Parents of children who have a special need and who are taught on a level of 'Hauptschule' can file an application for joint lessons at a Hauptschule. This is possible for the special focuses of seeing, hearing and communication, language, emotional and social development as well as physical and motor development."*(Bildungsministerium des Landes NRW 2014). The shift towards inclusion in German schools translates as a substantial change to the German school system, that continues to spark much public debate and raises questions about teacher education and preparedness to promote inclusive practices in their regular classrooms.

2.5 Inclusion: Australian Context

The way in which 'inclusion' is framed in Australian conversations is as *"children with special needs"* (Sens 2008, S. 285). In Germany, 'inclusion' is referred to as *"people with disabilities"* (Sens 2008, S, 285). "Special needs" can mean many things, and are not restricted to just physical or mental disabilities: they also include children whose parents have a disability; children whose families identify as Aboriginal, as well as those children from different cultural backgrounds (Send

2008, S. 285). Alongside mainstream Australian schools, there are 'special' schools that cater for *"children [with] multiple and serious disabilities."(Sens 2008, S. 285).* History reports that the parents of children with 'multiple and serious disabilities' that have challenged the education system and fought to have their child educated in a mainstream school, have won as they argue that mainstream schools are able to meet the needs of their child. Regardless, parents have a choice of where to send their child: *"the Australian education system emphasises .. inclusion, on the other hand the parent's freedom of choice. This is what is special about the Australian education system." (Sens 2008, S. 286).*

In order for a school to meet the 'special needs' of a prospective student via funding and resource support, the child needs to prove their need through thorough paediatric and psychological assessments. The end-product is a label attached to the child's condition thereby qualifying for categories of funding support. It is important to highlight that depending upon the child's 'special need', it will attract a different label and thereby funding support. The process to determine the level of student need demands a vigorous file of evidence and documents for teachers to better prepare for the student: *"A precondition for this is establishing of a knowledge base for teachers concerning information about different various types of various initial positions for learning (such as second language acquisition), latest empirical findings of learning research, structural and financial help as well as a successful cooperation with parents and others."* (Sens 2008, S. 286).

In Australia it is common for teachers to have exact knowledge about child development, specifically about optimal learning and teaching. The individuality of the child remains the focus evidenced by the fact that every curriculum is developed individually and is based on the learning ability of the child.

Every child with a 'special need' will have an individual learning support programme tailored by their teacher in consultation with other para-professionals involved with the child e.g. speech therapist, paediatrician. For example, children whose first language is not English will study in the "Language other than English" (LOTE) program. These students are taught topics from other fields of education in their mother tongue. These children *"experience an appreciation of their [language] competences and initially monolingual children profit from native speakers when learning a second language."(Sens 2008, S. 288).* The focus therefore is not on a student's inability to speak a language of the country, but on acknowledging multilingualism as a valuable resource.

Inclusion in Australia involves a careful and precarious balance between individual needs and financial capabilities. All students with special needs in Australian schools attract a combination of shared mobile services in school districts, including counseling, behaviour support and resources. Sen (2008) comments that inclusion in Australia "is not about more financial resources than less inclusive countries but that the resources are more mobile." (Sens 2008, S. 289).

Implementation in Teacher Education
The following section explores the pre-service preparation teachers undertake to qualify as teachers. The focus will mainly be on the field "Early Childhood", meaning children aged between zero and eight years.

After four years of studying and finishing with a Bachelor's degree, teachers can teach in pre- and primary schools. This makes the transitions between school forms easier for teachers: *"The transition between pre-school and primary school is freer because classic elementary pedagogic concepts are also included in the first years."* (Sens 2008, S. 290).

Bachelor graduates can join an Honors and Masters programs, and afterwards study towards a Doctoral degree. This model is more research-oriented: *"By now there is a Professor of Early Childhood Education in every Australian State who has achieved this position through praxis."* (Sens 2008, S. 290).

Teacher training in Australia tends to have a strong focus on linking theory to practice. The importance of linking theory and practice becomes apparent when considering a teaching career in Australia as many academically educated teachers work alternating at a school and in the research and/or further education field. Another important aspect of teacher training in Australia is that of personal development: *"Pedagogic practice is always shaped by the attitude of the people involved."* (Sens 2008, S. 293). Although the role of the teacher is highly professional, one cannot ignore how personal views, values and norms may impact upon teacher classroom behaviour. At UNE, part of the teacher training involves the students interrogating their own values and upbringing as it is recognized that not everything that is pedagogically and politically desired [in the classroom] is automatically the view of the future teacher. The goal is not to change the views of the students, but to increase their awareness of any transference into the classroom.

An effective teacher does not work in isolation and needs to communicate with a variety of people in and outside the school community. An important group of people teachers need to speak to, are the parents of their students. Training teachers learn how to communicate appropriately with parents to promote seamless communication between the contexts of the classroom and home. This consistency in language strengthens the authority of those in both contexts and promotes consistency every student requires.

Inclusion in Australian classrooms are effective because not only is every child seen and supported as an individual, but also because teacher education prepares teachers theoretically and practically with an understanding of their personal strengths and weaknesses.

2.6 Summary and Future Recommendations

Comparing the concept of 'inclusion' in both German and Australian contexts reveals that teacher attitude underpins the degree of its success in the classroom. There is a difference in the tone and language used to describe students with special needs, and the schools in Germany and Australia: in Germany it is *"children with disabilities"*, and in Australia the term is *"children with special needs"*. In Germany, the schools are called "Förderschule" and no longer "Sonderschule" – "Sonder" derives from "sonderbar" meaning odd, weird, strange, peculiar; "Förder" means foster, promote, stimulate, support. Irrespective, a teacher who wishes to teach "Förderschule", still needs to study "Sonderpädagogik". A shift in the terminology would be an improvement to address any negative connotation surrounding special needs.

Since the ratification of the *UN Convention on the Rights of Persons with Disabilities*, Germany has committed to create conditions in their schools to promote inclusive practices.

Starting with the school year 2014/2015 parents of children with special needs can register their child at a regular school. However, what happens after that is not clearly regulated: *"Every child is entitled to being admitted to their closest primary school, choosing the school form in accordance with the intake capacity set by the school authorities, when the school authorities have not established a school catchment area for this school form (§ 46 Absatz 3 SchulG)"* (Schulministerium des Landes NRW 2014). Thus, school authorities can individually establish an intake capacity and when this capacity is full, parents have to choose another school. When no regular school can be found, the parents have no choice but to send their child to a "Förderschule" in order to comply with certain criteria, such as a minimum number of pupils (Schulministerium des Landes NRW 2014).

There are also many more views and concepts in Australia that are worth exploring for the German context. The practice that children with a different cultural background attract additional support is something that the German school system does not practice. Children, whose mother tongue is not German, are taught in a single class at a "Hauptschule", without any differentiation of age or previous school career. This may lead to a child who still needs to learn the alphabet sitting next to a child who has a proficiency level of a regular class but only lacks German vocabulary. If Germany was to adopt the 'Language Other Than English' (LOTE) program, the children could learn from each other – language, culture and class topics at the same time, and this collaborative practice may prevent many prejudices and discriminations.

2.7 Conclusion

The focus of German teacher education may benefit from adopting a more holistic view of the child and the classroom as practiced in the Australian context. Viewing a child holistically means to appreciate all aspects of the child including individual special needs, and their personal and cultural background. In German schools, they recognize that even without an attested special need, not every child is able to successfully negotiate everyday school life. In response, the employment of Social Workers in schools supports these students. In order to improve this relationship however, the Social Workers need to appreciate the demands and pressures of the classroom teacher and special needs teacher, and vice versa, to provide a seamless and consistent level of support. Often the Social Workers are employed on temporary contracts that are ultimately disruptive and hindering to promoting consistency. Based on the current teacher education preparation, teachers for regular schools lack the training needed in special needs education, so the pragmatic question for the shift towards inclusive practices next year would be How will this work? Although some classes will have an additional special needs teacher or other professional, this may not be possible for every class. There are no concrete and binding statements regarding the realistic inclusion process, but maybe these problems and challenges need to occur in order for the politicians to understand that a change in society and the school system is long overdue.

2.8 References

Bardmann, T. M. (2008) Integration und Inklusion - systemtheoretisch buchstabiert: Neue Herausforderungen für die soziale und pädagogische Arbeit. In: Ytterhus, Borgunn / Kreuzer, Max: „Dabeisein ist nicht alles." Inklusion und Zusammenleben im Kindergarten, München: Reinhardt, S. 53-70.

Haug, P. (2008). Inklusion als Herausforderung der Politik im internationalen Kontext. In: Ytterhus, Borgunn / Kreuzer, Max: „Dabeisein ist nicht alles." Inklusion und Zusammenleben im Kindergarten, München: Reinhardt, S. 36-49.

Sens, A. (2008). Inklusion im Elementarbereich und Konzepte der Ausbildung – Entwicklungen in Australien. In: Ytterhus, Borgunn / Kreuzer, Max: „Dabeisein ist nicht alles." Inklusion und Zusammenleben im Kindergarten, München: Reinhardt, S. 283-297.

Schulministerium des Landes NRW (2013-2014), Bildungsportal, http://www.schulministerium.nrw.de/docs/Schulsystem/Schulformen/Foerderschule/Foerderschwerpunkte/index.html Zugegriffen 19.02.2014

Schulministerium des Landes NRW (2013-2014), Bildungsportal,http://www.schulministerium.nrw.de/docs/Schulsystem/Inklusion/FAQ/index.html Zugegriffen 19.02.2014

http://www.schulministerium.nrw.de/docs/Schulsystem/Inklusion/FAQ/FAQ-Konvention/index.html Zugegriffen 19.02.2014

http://www.schulministerium.nrw.de/docs/Schulsystem/Inklusion/FAQ/FAQ-Konvention/index.html Zugegriffen 19.02.2014

Statista, 2014, online verfügbar' http://de.statista.com/statistik/daten/studie/150660/umfrage/oeffentliche-gesamtausgaben-fuer-bildung---top-10-nach-eu-staat/ Zugegriffen 27.05.2014

Technische Universität Dortmund, 2014, http://www.dokoll.tu-dortmund.de/cms/labg2009/de/bachelor/sp/index.html (zuletzt abgerufen am 15.06.2014) http://www.dokoll.tu-dortmund.de/cms/labg2009/de/bachelor/sp/studienaufbau/index.html Zugegriffen 15.06.2014

University of New England, 2013, https://my.une.edu.au/courses/2014/courses/BEDECP/program-of-study.html Zugegriffen 02.06.2014

https://my.une.edu.au/courses/2014/courses/BEDECP Zugegriffen 02.06.2014

Hayley Matas and Ingrid Harrington
3 The Role of Parents, Teachers and Social Workers in the German and Australian Education Systems

3.1 Abstract

Inclusivity is the fundamental right of every student enrolled in New South Wales (NSW) government Primary and/or Secondary schools in Australia (Cologon 2013, p.11). This chapter compares the German Primary and Secondary educational systems against the equivalent New South Wales settings through an 'inclusive practice' lens. The data comprises the roles and perspectives of inclusion from Parents, Teachers, School Social Workers in German schools and School Counselors in Australian schools. This paper contextualizes both NSW and German education systems, and reports the significant findings and points of difference that may be used to inform current educational practices in NSW.

3.2 Introduction

The Public and private Primary and Secondary schools in Australia and Germany have varying definitions of what 'inclusion' is as applied to their educational settings. In 1997 all Australian schools adopted a 'full inclusion' policy which meant that all students deemed to have 'special educational needs' would "be educated in mainstream schools, alongside their peers in order for the benefits of inclusion to be realised" (Forbes 2007, p. 67). 'Inclusion' in the German educational setting refers to 'more open forms of teaching and learning' to ensure that all students are learning and have no disadvantage in the classroom (European Agency for Special Needs and Inclusive Education, n.d., p. 1). Recent changes to German teaching pedagogies that promote inclusive education practices include

"learning in groups of different levels, teaching with different objectives, weekly schedules, learning by doing, and learning with all the senses" (European Agency for Special Needs and Inclusive Education n.d., p. 1).

Inclusion or Integration?
The terms 'inclusion' and 'integration' are often used interchangeably despite significant differences between the two terms. Harman's research (2002, p. 1) suggests that the process of 'inclusion' focuses on helping all students meeting their needs in the mainstream classroom through the use of additional supports and/or adaptations.Additionally, Foreman (2005) suggests that the focus on effective inclusive practices asks *how* student needs can be met in the mainstream classroom. Inclusion, 'whilst it leads to integration' (Harman 2002, p. 1-2) goes beyond education and into the wider community, where individuals are accepted regardless of their cultural, ethnic, racial or social background.

Dependent upon the nature of the special need, the student may need to access Specialists or Learning Support teachers either in or external to the mainstream classroom. 'Integration' refers to the process of moving children from special education settings into the mainstream classroom where they undertake most, if not all, of their schooling (Ashman & Elkins, 2012, p.401). Being aware of the difference between inclusion and integration is vital as this research explores to identify whether 'integration', 'inclusion', or both are used in German schools.

For the purpose of this chapter within the contexts of the Australian and German Education systems:
- 'Inclusive practice' "recognises individual different gifts and abilities, and provides opportunities for all individuals to succeed" (Evans, 2007, p. 6);
- the school's role in the implementation of inclusive practices is to "create a learning environment where barriers to learning are avoided wherever possible" (Evans 2007, p. 6); and,

- "Integration" in schools means viewing the individual student as a 'whole' person and ensuring they 'fit' into their school setting and social groups. In order for integration and inclusion to successfully occur, it is vital that every person in the school appreciates difference and respect each other, regardless of each individual culture, religious beliefs and/or disabilities (Fan 2004). This paper will discuss what the NSW Education system can learn from the southwest German Education system, and what changes would need to be made to the Australian system to parallel the role of parents and School Social Workers in the school day.

3.3 Literature Review

3.4 The NSW Education System

In 1980 NSW government schools saw a greater focus on identifying and meeting the needs of student mental health in schools. A *School-Link Initiative* (NSW

DEC, n.d, p. 1) launched in 1999 by the NSW Government focused upon Australian Universities making Psychology units available to Education students, and the adoption of a Whole-School ethos "to improve the mental health of children, adolescents and young people in NSW schools" (Urbis, 2011, p. 74). The *School-Link initiative* aimed to identify, manage and support mental health issues students may be experiencing at school, and empower the school community with a greater understanding of the mental health issues young people face through improved knowledge, collaborative practices internal and external to the school community, and skill development.

According to Forbes (2007, p. 67), the concept of an "inclusive school" is a process where "everyone belongs, is accepted, and where students with special education needs are supported and cared for by their peers and other members of the school community".

In broad and global terms, the World Health Organization in the International Classification of Functioning, Disability and Health (ICF) defines a 'Disability' as an umbrella term for any impairment, activity limitation, or participation restriction (http://www.who.int/classifications/icf/en/). In New South Wales, the term *'Students with a Disability or Additional Learning Needs'* (NSW DEC 2013) refers to students who "may require additional support at some time in their schooling due to a disabling condition" (NSW DEC 2013). It is important to note that a learning *disability* and learning *difficulty* are two categories catered for under the same NSW DEC policy, although they are quite different in nature. A *difficulty* is defined as *one or more of 17 limitations, restrictions or impairments which have lasted or are likely to last, for a period of six months or more, and which restrict a person's everyday activities* (Australian Institute of Health and Welfare 2013, p. 1). Whilst a learning *disability* is defined in the Australian *Commonwealth Disability Discrimination Act_1992 as a disorder or malfunction which results in the person learning differently from a person without the disorder or malfunction* (Kerridge 2008, p. 1).

What is key in the two definitions is the premise that the issues a learning *difficulty* presents can be ameliorated with the right supports, personnel and time, whereas the diagnosis and inherent issues associated with a particular learning *disability* are unlikely to change i.e. the disability itself will never go away, even though its symptoms and characteristics may be effectively managed to support learning.As mainstream schools cater for students with a learning difficulty and a learning disability, the distinction between the terminology of 'difficulty' and 'disability' are highly significant for the NSW DEC funding model. The student 'status' as determined by the school with directly impact upon the type, amount and frequency of support the student will be eligible for during their time at school. The impact of the DEC's Inclusion policy has meant that students with disabilities and/or learning difficulties can be enrolled into mainstream schools and mainstream classes. In recognition of the number of students meeting the DEC's definition and parameters of what they deem to be learning *difficulties* and learning *disabilities*, the NSW State Department of Education and Communities (DEC) increased their expenditure in NSW government schools by 76% in the period of 2009-2011 (Urbis 2011, p. 50).

The New South Wales Board of Studies (NSW BOS) that regulates teacher training standards in embracing the new Inclusion policy directs that:(a) all students must be able to engage in, take responsibility for and continue their own learning; (b) all students are entitled to a core of knowledge, skills, understanding and values; (c) education must be inclusive of all students attending school in NSW; and, (d) teachers, schools and school authorities will decide how to maximise students' learning. (NSW Board of Studies: K-10 Curriculum Framework, 2002)

The choice of pedagogy open for teachers has been enhanced in light of the *Disability Standards for Education* (2005) and the *Disability Discrimination Act* (1992) guidelines. In recognition of these important documents, the DEC implemented a program called the *Special Education Initiative* (2006-2007) that aimed to "meet the challenges of special needs" of students in all NSW government Primary and Secondary schools. The impact the *Disability Standards for Education* (2005), and the *Disability Discrimination Act* (1992) had on mainstream school enrolments meant that for the first time, parents could enroll their child into a NSW school of their choice (Dixon and Verenikina, 2007). The support provided to students with disabilities and/or learning difficulties in mainstream classes varied depending upon what their needs were, and what the school was able to offer. Most typically, students with special learning needs were taught in the mainstream classroom with mainstream students, and with the 1:1 or shared support of a Teacher's Aide. There were other students whose learning and social needs were so great that within the mainstream school structure, they were enrolled into a support class with similar students, and they participated in the mainstream class with support for certain subjects. It is now expected that all teachers in NSW will teach students with a disability and/or a learning difficulty in their mainstream classroom. A consequence of several changes at the Federal and State government levels saw the funding of Teacher Aide's (TA) or Support teachers in mainstream schools come under much scrutiny. Applications from school Principals, parents or para-professionals for TA support for individual students became more complex, competitive and the demand to justify the need was high. Consequently, as the numbers of students requiring TA support in the mainstream classroom increased, the numbers of TA's decreased or remained the same. By way of illustration, five years ago in a mainstream classroom where there were two students with a disability and five with learning difficulties requiring TA support, there would have been two full time dedicated TA's providing up to six hours of support for these students. In today's classroom for the same seven students, there would be one TA providing support for these students collectively for two hours per day.

NSW schools have access to School Counselors (SC) that work with students, parents and teachers to provide counseling and psychological assessment of students with special needs. To be employed as a SC, the person must have an Education degree, and undertake additional training. The role of SC's in NSW schools is to provide

"counseling service; work in consultation with other staff members to improve student learning and wellbeing; carry out cognitive, social, emotional and behavioural assessments of students; contribute to the development of and planning for students with special needs; and refer students and their families onto the other agencies and support services that may be required to support health and wellbeing for the student and their families" (NSW DEC n.d, p. 3).

Due to economic rationalism, a cluster of 6-8 schools may share the same SC in one region that translates that a SC may spend one or part of a day, once a week, at a school. As such, they are in great demand and highly transient in their work nature, as It is uncommon for schools to have a dedicated SC based at the school. SC's work across Primary and Secondary schools with students from preschool to year 12 (NSW DEC, 2013).

The New South Wales Education system consists of children attending school from Kindergarten to Year 12 (K-12). Primary school begins at Kindergarten and finishes in Year 6, and the seven years are scaffolded into three 'Stages': K, 1,2 = Stage 1; 3-4 = Stage 2, and 5-6 = Stage 3. The Stage structure provides teachers with the flexibility to differentiate the curriculum for a broader student ability/age range, hence the introduction of 'combined' classrooms eg. a 1/2, or 5/6 class that has a mixture of both students enrolled in both grades. Upon completion of Primary school, students progress to Secondary school to complete Years 7 to 12. Again, the secondary system has a continuation of the Stage system with years 7-8 = Stage 4; 9-10 = Stage 5, and 11-12 = Stage 6.

Unlike the German Education System, there is no formal recognition and segregation for students based on vocational trajectory in Secondary school. All students have an option at the completion of Year 10 to leave secondary school with a 'Year 10 Certificate' and attend other learning opportunities eg. Technical and Further Education (TAFE), workplace apprenticeships, etc. Those students that complete Year 12 graduate with a Higher School Certificate (HSC) and an Australian Tertiary Admissions Rank (ATAR) score out of 100 that is used by tertiary institutions to offer further study in particular courses. A student's ATAR score is calculated by adding together a student's best 10 units of study to give a score out of 500. The score is then converted to a percentage, scaled against all other Year 12 students in that year, which results in an individual's ATAR score. Hence, an ATAR is based on rank, not student performance per se e.g. if a student receives an ATAR score of 80, it means they have performed better than 80% of students, hence they are in the top 20% of Year 12 students in that year. An example would be a student wishing to study Veterinary Science would need an A-TAR score of 93 and above, whilst a student wishing to pursue an Education degree would require an ATAR score of 71. Governments are now de-regulating the university system and not supporting as many placements per degree. The ramifications of the government action were that every university has now become its own business, needing to attract and retain students to earn an income. In reality, the competitiveness of degree entrance scores soars higher as universities tend to offer placements to students presenting with the higher ATAR score. So whilst many students wishing to pursue an Education degree may meet the ATAR score of 71/100, due to the higher competitive nature, the university will make offers and fill its annual quota of Education placements to students who present with ATAR scores over 80. In the 1980's tertiary education was free, however due to government policies, to study a tertiary degree in today's terms is costly as the student is required to pay for each unit. Again, depending upon which area of study, each unit attracts different costs: the average cost of a unit in Veterinary Science is approximately $3500-$5,000 each, whilst the average cost of a unit in an Education award ranges from $700-850.

There has been an on-going discussion between educational academics, school educators, and the DEC on how to improve teacher responses and promotion of effective inclusive practices in the classroom. Claims from parents that there were practicing teachers that could not effectively spell and calculate mathematical sums broadened the focus on teacher quality and training. In an effort to identify areas contributing to ineffective teacher practices, the Gillard government (2010-2013) made links to tertiary teaching placements being offered to Yr 12 students that lacked abilities in literacy and numeracy, as an area needing attention. In response, her government mandated that all students – Yr 12 and mature age - wishing to pursue a B.Ed.Primary degree needed to receive a minimum overall Australian Tertiary Admissions Rank (ATAR) score of 70/100, and demonstrate Band 4 (marks ranging between 70-79) in Yr 12 English and Mathematics. Despite these requirements, the NSW Teacher regulating body, the Board of Studies, Teaching & Educational Standards (BOSTES) were not satisfied that these measures had gone far enough to ensure teacher quality. In July 2015 they mandated that all students interested in pursuing a B.Ed.Primary degree must now i) pass an independent tertiary entrance exam that focuses on their literacy and numeracy abilities; and ii) need to demonstrate Band 5 (marks ranging between 80-89) in three Year 12 subjects including English, Mathematics, and one other. It is too early to gauge how effective these measures will be in producing educators that respond more appropriately to students and promote inclusive practices more successfully. It does reflect however, that governments recognize the importance of a multi-faceted approach in order to demonstrate effectual pedagogical and inclusive practices in the mainstream classroom.

Generally speaking, parents and students are free to choose which secondary school they attend, be it private or government. To better inform parents of what school offers in academic, social, sporting, vocational and creative curriculas, the NSW DEC introduced an online website called '*mySchool*'. At this site, parents can nominate or explore which school would be the best 'fit' for their child's abilities and vocation. The site reports figures and averages on how the school performed in academic, social, sporting, vocational and creative curriculas when compared to each other. It became obvious soon after the launch of the *mySchool* website, that enrolment at certain government schools became highly popular at the expense of other schools that didn't rate so well in comparison. In response to this, the DEC began a stricter approach to enforcing geographical zoning to eligibility to attend a certain Secondary school. Unless an exceptional case could be made for their child's needs, parents were now required to send their child to the Secondary school in their zone. If the school was still unacceptable to the parent for whatever reason, a common practice had been that families would move house into the required zone, or consider sending their child into a Private school. Private education is expensive in Australia with Primary school fees averaging from $8,000-10,000 per year, and Secondary school fees averaging $20,000 – 35,000 per year. As these school fees are out of reach for the average family, there is immense pressure on government schools to deliver a quality education to all its students.

3.5 The German Education System

The implementation of the German education system varies throughout Germany as each Region decides upon their own educational policies. It is common practice for most children to attend Primary school, or '*Grundschule*' from the age of 6 to 10. Upon completion of *Grundschule*, students are streamed into a Secondary school depending upon their vocational and academic ability.

The three main types of Secondary schools available for students are:
1) ***Gymnasium*** – designed to prepare students for tertiary university education after completing their final school examination, known as the '*Abitur*' in grade 12.
2) ***Realschule*** – caters for academically intermediate students and finishes with a final examination, known as the '*Mittlere Reife*' for the students after grade 10.
3) ***Hauptschule*** – known as the least academic of schools, prepares the students for vocational education and training, after completing an examination after grade 9 or 10.

Less than five years ago, the German education system did not support students with special needs in their mainstream schools. Students diagnosed with learning difficulties and/or learning disabilities attended Special Schools known as *'Förderschule'* or *'Sonderschule'*. As the concept of 'Special Education' and 'Inclusive Education' became an accepted practice in schools globally, the *Förderschulen* and *Sonderschulen* became the subject of much criticism for essentially discriminating and separating students with a disability and/or learning difficulties from mainstream school classes. Interestingly, the collected data reflected a small number of students diagnosed with a disability and/or learning difficulty, currently being mainstreamed in *Hauptschulen* and *Gymnasien*. The shift away from the practice of enrolling students with a disability and/or learning difficulties into Special Schools out to the mainstream classroom has however, resulted in limited options for these parents, specifically a loss of financial support provided by the government. It is for this reason why the transition of students with special needs into the mainstream classroom has been well orchestrated so as to disadvantage no one.

The concept of 'Inclusion' in German schools is best described as "every child is to be appreciated in their individuality and diversity as an enrichment for successful learning for all students" (Klemm 2012, p. 1). Parents, Teachers and School Social Workers that support the concept of inclusion believe there is no need for students with a disability and/or learning difficulties to be isolated or segregated into groups, advocating that the needs of all students can be met in the mainstream classroom. German schools supporting an inclusive learning environment report that students without special needs benefit from learning with students with special needs in their class as they "develop greater social skills" (Klemm 2012, p. 1).

German schools do not advocate a school uniform or dress code that enables students to wear casual dress. An argument often associated with a 'no uniform' policy is that it can facilitate student bullying and judgment from other students based on the choice and 'trendiness' of clothes. During the data collection I did not observe this practice nor was it reported or discussed by interviewed school staff as being an on-going issue.

3.6 Comparison of the German and Australian education systems

Examining the educational systems of Germany and NSW, Australia, it is evident that there exist similarities and differences between practices held at Australian and German schools.

Some differences include:

German educational system	Australian educational system
Students streamed based on their *academic ability*	Students streamed based on their *special needs*
School Social Workers are key staff based in schools. They are more involved in the students' social and family problems, and able to contact students outside of school hours and initiate home visits to the student and their family.	*School Counselors* are shared amongst schools and do not formally explore the environments external to school. They are limited to supporting the student using only school-based resources within school times.
Parents and teachers work together to determine the school-day events for every student	Parents and teachers may consult about individual students but not for the whole class

Table 3-1

Some similarities include:

German educational system	Australian educational system
Have distinct Primary - *Grundschule'* (K-6) and Secondary (7-12) - *Gymnasium, Realschule, Hauptschulabschluss* stages of school.	Have distinct Primary (K-6) and Secondary (7-12) stages of school.
School Social Workers provide support services such as counseling, intervention and academic assistance for the students attending the school.	*School Counselors* provide support services such as counseling, intervention and academic assistance for the students attending the school.
Have the *Hauptschulabschluss* from Year 10 where students can pursue vocational careers.	Have the *Technical and Further Education (TAFE)* system from Year 10 where students can pursue vocational careers.

Table 3-2

The main difference between the two systems appears to be the full time, on-campus appointment of School Social Workers as permanent staff in German Schools. In the NSW system, schools share School Counselors who would be the closest equivalent in nature i.e. non-teaching. The School Social Worker's parameters being firmly set within the School Social Work discourse, and the School Counselor's parameters set within an Educational framework. According to the Australian Government Department of Health Services (2013, p. 1), the role of a School Social Worker in Australia is to "support and assist in the form of short-term counseling, exploration of options and providing information", which is identical for School Social Workers employed in German Schools. Whilst the definition is the same for both countries, only Germany base their Social Workers in schools.

3.7 Methodology

The research was conducted by a qualified Australian Primary school teacher deemed as a 'Beginning Teacher' i.e. a teacher working within the first five years since graduation. She worked with a team of three German Social Work students enrolled at the Fachhochschule Dortmund. Together as a team, they entered four German schools, observed the school day and interviewed some of the staff, specifically teachers and School Social Workers.

The research focused primarily on three Primary schools and one sencondary school.One of the key reasons why these schools were chosen was because they accepted students with disabilities and/or learning difficulties into their mainstream classes. Due to the Australian researcher's inability to speak German, the research team then met at the end of each data gathering session to discuss and share what they had learnt about each of the schools visited. Additionally, due to the limited time frame of two weeks to collect the data from schools, it was decided to utilize a range of data collection methods, namely Classroom Observations, and Semi-structured, informal interviews. Data collection from a variety of sources allows for consistency, improved accuracy and understanding of the study's findings (McCrady, Ladd, Vermont and Steele, 2010) as triangulation amongst the data can occur.

Student privacy and confidentiality were protected as the names of participants were not provided to the researchers, and no direct photos were taken of the students.

The Semi-structured interviews allowed the questions to be structured according to the purpose of the research paper, and the open-ended questions allowed for more descriptive answers (Opdenakker, 2006, p.1). The technique of Classroom observation was also used as it was easy and quick to do and provided a living 'snap-shot' of a typical day. It was important to ensure that the observers i.e. the researchers, remained invisible as possible to ensure the students acted typically (Russ-Eft & Preskill, 2009).

Classroom Observations

The bulk of the data collection was conducted through observations of the students participating in their regular classes. All Classroom observations proceeded by taking notes on the students' behaviour and attitude to learning, and their ability to complete work independently in a student-centered learning environment. The variables that were considered for the different observations included the a) time of day the students were observed, b) gender, c) task requirements, d) the subject being observed, e) the ability of the student as indicated by the classroom teacher and f) distractions that existed in the classroom.

Majority of the lessons observed were English lessons that were taught in English. This was fortunate for the Australian researcher to understand the lesson content, and involved the students learning the alphabet or asking and responding to basic questions in English.

Observation notes were taken on how the students worked in the classroom and their reactions to teacher instructions. This was fundamental to the study because in order to see what role the School Social Worker played in the students' school day, it was essential to gain an understanding of how the students preferred to learn and be engaged in class. The observations were guided by numerous questions about the German School System including:

- Were the students always on task? When were they not on task?
- Did the students choose work at an appropriate level to challenge them?
- Were the students actively engaging with their peers with their learning, or did they always work independently?
- What direction and facilitation did the teacher provide for students to self-direct their own learning?
- Did the students look satisfied with their work? Note- the purpose of this question was to see whether the students were satisfied with the work they were producing. As most of work was student-centered, it was important to observe whether the student rushed through tasks to receive achievement rewards or positive praise, or whether they put all of their effort into completing their work to the best of their ability.
- Did any problems exist with having students with diverse needs in one class? If so, what were they? How are they catered for?

Other observations took place watching the School Social Workers interact with students out of the formal classroom time e.g. as the School Social Worker was showing the research team around the school at recess and lunch. By observing the student's interaction and body language with the School Social Workers, it was evident that they had a high level of respect and were comfortable with each School Social Worker.

3.7.1 Semi-structured, informal interviews

Informal, semi-structured interviews were used as they provided direct answers and scope to the open-ended questions posed by the researcher (Roulston 2012, p.12). A semi-structured interview according to Longhurst (2010, p. 103) is a "verbal interchange where one person, the interviewer, attempts to elicit information from another person by asking questions". One of the strengths of this type of interview is that it offers the "participants the chance to explore issues they feel are important" (Longhurst 2010, p. 103). The semi-structured nature of the interviews also provided the School Social Workers a 'space' in which to elaborate on the questions. According to Roulston (2012, p. 12), the open-ended nature of questions allow "interviewees to formulate answers in their own words concerning topics specified by the interviewer".

Due to research planning protocols such as organising permission for students to be interviewed and time constraints in arranging appointments with schools and Social Workers, no students were interviewed during this research project, only the School Social Workers and the Teachers were interviewed. The privacy and confidentiality of the School Social Workers interviewed was protected through the school's direct connection with the Fachhochschule Dortmund. The interviews lasted approximately one hour and were taped and fully transcribed in English. The interviews took place during school hours in the School Social Worker's office or the Staff common room located at the school.
The following semi-structured interview schedule was used for the School Social Workers at the Primary and Secondary schools:
- Describe what your role as a Social Worker entails at this school, and how does it support students and teachers?
- How often do you meet with the classroom teachers to discuss student matters? What sorts of things would you typically discuss with these teachers?
- How do you support the classroom teacher in their teaching?

- Do you believe that some students respond better to you rather than the classroom teacher? Why do you think this is? Describe these sorts of students.
- Describe some of the most popular and successful strategies you have used in the classroom when working with students. What strategies you would recommend to other teachers to adopt for an inclusive classroom? Do your strategies focus on specific small changes in the daily routine of a student, or do they impact more broadly in a whole-school approach?
- Describe the different types of special needs students that present in your classroom? How many students do you have with disabilities when compared to those with learning difficulties in your classroom?
- What strategies do you use to cater for individual student needs? Is this for students with or without a disability/learning difficulty?
- How do you as a Social Worker encourage and promote quality engagement and participation amongst students?
- What sorts of things do students discuss with you? How does it help you support the student in the classroom?
- What training is most needed to equip school staff to work with special needs students and their individual requirements? Discuss some examples of successful training.

An advantage of visiting the schools with the other German members of the research project was that it allowed for on-going discussions amongst ourselves. It also provided an opportunity for us to compare our different observations at each school, such as how they catered for students with a disability/learning difficulty, the services available to the students at the school, and what choice of pedagogy the teacher's chose to teach the curriculum. As the Australian researcher did not understand nor speak German, it was necessary for translation to occur so that it could be understood between all parties. Nes, Abma, Jonsson and Deeg (2010, p. 1) explain how "language is central in all phases ranging from data collection, to analysis and representation". The research team of the three German researchers and the one Australian researcher met at the end of each school visit for one hour to discuss the day's data collection. This was valuable as it acted as a form of debriefing and ensured that all information was shared between members. This process helped reduce the likelihood of misinterpreting or misrepresenting the data.

3.7.2 Choice of schools

Four schools were chosen for this research because they all had a connection with the Fachhochschule Dortmund's research on Inclusive Education, had employed School Social Workers on staff, and had implemented a range of inclusive strategies to cater for their students. The culturally diverse staff and student populations warmly welcomed the concept of 'inclusion' in the schools.

The data collected from the four German schools was conducted through five separate one-hour interviews with the School Social Workers, each based at one of the three Primary schools, and one Secondary school. Two or three researchers were present at each interview that was recorded and transcribed to ensure that each researcher was able to access the interview for accuracy when writing this research project.

3.8 Demographic Profiles

3.8.1 School A (Primary)

The *school A* is an inclusive school that promotes inclusive practices for students to develop their talents and needs at their own pace. The school strives to support independent learning and social competency, promote lateral thinking, and encourages creativity. They believe that a school system in which children are taught together regardless of their disability, learning disability or other characteristic, is essential. Furthermore, the school respects the individual needs of each student, their own opinions and flexibility in the design of school life enabling each child to achieve their own success.

The school does not have a Social Worker based at the school but is staffed by four Educational Specialists and four Teachers that design and implement student programs. The team of staff keeps the school operating smoothly as a small community. Without a school-based Social Worker the school relies heavily on communication between all staff about the students. The teaching staff meet regularly each week for an hour to share this information, and the four Educational Specialists encourage the teachers and give them advice on how to best meet the needs of any students with disabilities they may have in their classroom. The school encourages parental involvement in the school life by having an open start time, where parents can spend time with their child at the school (Teacher school A) One inclusive concept for the school is the idea of a "morning circle" (Teacher school A) where students sit together with a "speaker ball" indicating who will talk at each set time.

The school has many physical features purpose-built to cater for all student needs, such as stairs, ramps and elevators. The school has a fully equipped kitchen staffed with a Chef who prepares the students' daily lunches, and a communal student lunchroom where the students eat lunch together as a group, or 'snacks' at their own leisure. The school has several purpose-built rooms to help the students expand their creativity including an art room, woodwork room, building block and toy room, and a 3D sensory room. There is no designated Teacher in these rooms, and students have minimal supervision when they engage in these optional activities at any time. A teacher may walk in occasionally to make sure students are on-task and safe.

The *school A* was familiar with people coming to observe lessons as it was classified as an "Inclusive" school. The school believed an observation time limit of four hours would result in minimum distractions to the students, so all observations needed to occur within that timeframe. In order to observe first hand how the school and the teachers responded to the requirements of those students identified with special needs, for the purposes of this research, the teacher shared the nature of the special need certain students had prior to observing them in the classroom. The observations occurred in mainstream classes that included students with special needs, and the teacher made us aware of the special needs students prior to observing the lesson. By doing this, it was possible to observe their interactions with others and how they managed to engage with the required classroom tasks. It also provided the opportunity to observe how the teacher adapted different teaching styles for these students.

The combined Grade 1 to 3 class observed at the *school A* consisted of four teachers, two teachers per classroom working with a combined total of 25 students. It was observed that many classes proceeded with students sitting on the floor, rather than in the typical 'desk-like' structure. The classroom only had one table with seven chairs for the students to sit on, even though there were 25 students in the class. The day progressed around a structure where students could choose between what subject type or project they wished to work on within the predetermined time-frame. The teacher's role was more of a facilitator to the student's learning, rather than as an educator: they spoke in a calm, soft tone encouraging the students to solve the higher order problems and open-ended questions in their activities and projects. The concept of 'individualised learning', where "the learner is placed at the centre of teaching, learning and assessment", (Fullan, Hill and Crevola, 2006; Keamy, Nicholas, Mahar, & Herrick, 2007; Leadbeater, 2005 as cited in Jones & McLean, 2012, p. 2) is emphasised as the students do not receive reports or grades reflecting their progress based on regular assessment, rather the teacher has regular interviews with the students informing them of the areas they are succeeding and areas where improvement is required. The school chooses to monitor student learning by breaking the students into groups of eight every week. They are then instructed by the one teacher who closely monitors the learning progress of these eight students, and writes individual learning plans and daily task registers, showing what each student has done for the day on each of the students in the group.

3.8.2 School B (Primary)

The *school B* Primary promotes an inclusive education philosophy in city surroundings. The school interprets "inclusive education" as providing "individual, learning objectives, differentiated work for all students" . (School social worker school B) The *school B* school has 23 students in each of their classes, a total of 23 teachers, including one Special Education Teacher and one School Social Worker employed at the school. The students are able to participate in workshops of their choice including sports, drama and dance, to cater for the parents who work shift hours and evenings.

The *school B* had students ranging from grades 1-4 combined into a classroom with one classroom teacher, and other support staff present in the classroom at different points in time. The school would engage local community volunteers to be Teacher Aides in the classroom to offer assistance to all students, and deliver dance, drama, sport and music classes. The role of the support staff was to assist the classroom teacher in supporting students so that the teacher could effectively deliver the lesson. The support staff was able to provide support the classroom teacher by providing group and/or individual support for students with behavioural problems, learning disabilities and/or difficulties.

The school promotes having everyone welcome as reflected in their motto "In the sense of an inclusive school, we welcome all people in our School!"(School Social Worker school B) . The school is disadvantaged in terms of funding as the city does not provide the school with "a helper for integration" (School Social Worker school B) in the classroom. The lack of funding received by the school is evident as teachers are responsible for the cleaning and maintenance of the school, and the volunteer nature of the Teacher's Aides and Support Staff.

A feature of the *school B* is that all students complete individual, differentiated work, although their classes are students from grades 1-4 combined. All of students at the school are separated for the subjects Maths and English depending on their grade ability, whereas every student determines which activity they want to complete at their own set ability level for all other subjects. A team consisting of Teachers, a Special Education teacher and a School Social Worker develop the curricula for the students. They construct and implement social, behavioural and academic support plans for each student. They collaborate to team-teach in support groups in the classroom for behavioural and academic support, and in the playground for social support so the teachers can monitor their progress. Team teaching helps "create a dynamic and interactive learning environment" (Leavitt 2006, p.1) and for the students, it pushes them to "achieve higher levels of integration in their study of new material" (Leavitt 2006, p.2). The teacher's role is one of a facilitator, encouraging students to complete their work, offering individual support where required, and motivating students to challenge themselves.

Programs implemented in this school are the traditions, rules and techniques of the school to be passed on to the younger students by the older students. The Mediator program was implemented by the school's Social Worker. The program trains students to act as mediators in the playground and in the classrooms. They are taught "specific knowledge and practicing skills of mediators, games and exercises to encourage self-esteem, cognition and naming of feelings and cooperation"(School Social Worker school B) . The students complete an examination to ensure the students are aware of their roles. The school insists that "learning together from each other is paramount" (School Social Worker school B) and this enables the classroom teacher and support staff to act as a 'consultant' and have more time to work with the individual children.

The Role of the Social Worker

The *school B* has one school-based Social Worker and her role is primarily to support both parents and students into the school community. Typical to the geographical area, many families identify as Turkish and they experience a low socio-economic status. These families rely on the School Social Worker to provide them with information and assistance on living in Germany, including access to financial support services to help the students and their families adjust to life in Germany.

3.8.3   Primary Schools

In 2011, public schools supported the employment of full-time School Social Workers into the primary and secondary school staff community. Prior to this, it was uncommon for School Social Workers to be a part schools as schools did not have the funding nor resources to employ them. The implementation of full-time Social Workers based at the school was prompted by the high influx of refugees to Koln, and their employment was dependent upon the funding received from the Government for each Region.

The local school system was unable to sufficiently support these students and their families as they experienced the hardship and transition of immigration, whilst concurrently integrating their children into the school. For example, not all students were able to comprehend different courses being taught across different times and in some cases different languages. Most immigrant children were unable to speak German or English, which were the main languages used in German schools. The role of the Social Workers was to a) support students and their families, b) to provide financial support, c) make families aware of the support services available, and d) to support the students who came from broken families or single-parent families.

3.8.4 School C (Primary)

The *school C is a* Primary School, staffed by teachers, a Special Education Teacher and a School Social Worker. The *school C* supports an inclusive school by accepting all students and helping them to "develop personal, social and physical skills in an ever-changing society" (*Schoolprogramm school C*) Additionally, the *school* supports individualised learning through organising an individual weekly schedule, including learning tasks according to the level of each child and through group work.

The school has a Special Education Unit consisting of a group of four to five students who work together with a classroom teacher on elementary levels of English and Maths problems, and daily living skills. The children involved in the Special Education Unit have very limited language barriers as they have recently immigrated from Turkey, Greece and/or Poland. The school supports them in a number of ways including:
- employing teachers that speak their native language;
- allowing students who cannot cope with the full school day to go home early; and
- making exams optional and/or the school organises for appropriate support services i.e. a reader or writer, to ensure the student is given a fair advantage to perform well in the exam.

These students are withdrawn from their classes for an hour each day at different times depending on their grade level, and work in a small group of approximately five students with the Special Education teacher. When the Special Education Teacher is not working with these groups, she visits the classrooms of other students with special needs for two lessons per week to assist the classroom teacher. Collaboration is a big focus of the school, and the Special Education teacher works with the School Social Worker and classroom teacher in developing lessons and individual education plans for all students. Together, they set three goals for each student to achieve in approximately 6-8 weeks, and reward their achievements through a point system for good behaviour that may include students being exempt from homework. The classroom teacher believes that all students need constant positive praise and encouragement as it helps them to achieve their goals. The classroom teacher ensures that the goals the students set for themselves are attainable, and after each lesson the teacher adjusts the student's weekly points to reflect improvement, and determine if they qualify for the reward of not having to complete homework for that night.

The school C works hard to ensure that the family backgrounds of their students are included in the learning environment. An effective way in which they do this includes placing a world map on one of the school walls and identifying where students in their school originally came from, and identifying their cultural background. The School Social Worker works with both the students and their families as they try to build a sense of belonging and organisation into their lives. As refugee families, many may grapple with new circumstances and changes not experienced in their homeland e.g. unemployment, the loss of a male role model in their home, etc. To manage the challenges their new life in Germany may pose, the school's Social Worker visits the home regularly and offers professional support and advice on areas such as finding employment, obtaining financial help, and the range of services that are available for the family.

The Role of the Social Worker

The School Social Workers rely on a personal connection with the parents and students, as it is central to developing a sense of trust with the students so they can better relate to them. They regularly contact the student's parents via phone or a personal home visit to the family's home to discuss their child's progress and wellbeing The School Social Worker is highly involved in the day-to-day running of the classroom and discusses any issues with the classroom teachers to develop individual student action plans. The School Social Worker and classroom teachers are "very reliant on each other, to report issues, achievements and challenges". (School Social Worker school C) The School Social Worker has other roles within the school including, running their own lessons to students on how to best deal with stress and pressure, and how students can improve their Social skills. These lessons occur within the typical school day with the whole class within the moring lessons. These students are withdrawn from their regular lessons and either go into the office of the school Social Worker, or a classroom set aside in the school for the School Social Worker to work with the students. The School Social Worker can also withdraw 5-6 students and take them on a "dream journey', which incorporates 45 minutes of relaxation time on a waterbed, with dimmed lighting and soothing music.

The School Social Worker completes mandatory reporting to the State Protective Services on child abuse and also mediates any conflict and/or issues between students. The School Social Workers are required to be outside during classroom breaks and encouraged to play games and encourage positive social interactions between students. It is hoped that students will take the opportunity to talk to them during these informal times. Teachers and School Social Workers at the school maintain student confidentiality and privacy. The classroom teacher may not always know the family status and personal problems of students in their classes, and likewise, the school's Social Worker may not always be aware of the learning difficulties of the students they work with, it can be seen as "unnecessary knowledge" to her job as she already views each child as an individual (School Social Worker school C) . The following table summarises key aspects of the three Primary School classes:

The School Social Workers at each school would team-teach and at times work individually with students in class, or withdraw students for lessons in relation to 'Social studies'. 'Social studies' was a topic taught by a School Social Worker to help students gain appropriate social skills in terms of communicating and interacting with others. A responsibility the School Social Worker had was to assist students in developing and maintaining friendships with their peers by 'matching' students by their interests. They would pair students on a 1:1 basis or in small groups when the students were more confident talking to their peers. The School Social worker and would continue to build their social skills by leading fun brainstorming sessions that were designed to help students develop the courage and confidence to make their own friendships in the playground and in class.

'Dream' rooms

Two Primary schools, *school B* and school C offered 'relaxation' or 'dream' rooms where all students could lie down on a bed and/or on bean bags to sleep or rest during their recess and lunch breaks, individually or in small groups of up to six students. Additionally, the school's Social Workers were able to take students from their classes and work with them in the 'dream' rooms to teach students how to meditate and cope with stresses they may be experiencing. Students were able to use the rooms to go and sleep, particularly if their parents worked at night and they had the responsibility of looking after their younger siblings. In each of the schools, the maintenance of the 'dream' rooms were the School Social Worker's responsibility, and time spent in these rooms was always seen as a privilege for the students.

At the *school B*, the students were able to freely access the room at recess or lunch with up to six students in the room at any one time. Teacher Supervision was not required in this room, as the Teacher's staffroom was across the hallway and teachers could hear if there were any issues. The room was seen as a quiet resting room where students could escape from the busy playground atmosphere and relax during recess and lunch.

At the *School C*, the students had to be accompanied to the room by the Social Worker in groups because the room was isolated from their regular classrooms and the students needed the School Social Workers key to unlock the room and permission to be in there. This room was seen as a room for the Social Worker to work with the students and enable them to feel safe. Students were withdrawn from class and included in sessions where they would lay on a waterbed with dimmed lights, and the School Social Worker would guide these students through meditation to help them relax or overcome stresses or anxiety.

3.8.5 The Secondary School D

The *school* D has approximately 25 students in each of their classes, qualified teachers and two School Social Workers employed at the school. The school enrolls students from 10 years old to Grade 12 where they sit their final examination to receive a study offer at a university.

The *school D* was the only Secondary school chosen due to the limited time to collect data. The purpose of including a Secondary school in the research was to examine by comparison how the concept of inclusion manifests in a Secondary school setting when compared to the Primary setting. The school provided an opportunity for the researcher to observe how students recently transitioned from Primary school, were fitting in to the new Secondary school way of doing things.

Not all Secondary schools in Germany have School Social Workers, yet the *school D* had two School Social Workers due to its large student population of 1000 students.

This school supports the concept of 'inclusion', and although "disabled and non-disabled children are taught together in some classes e.g. in the cooking class,"there is only "one inclusion class" that runs for 12 lessons per week. (School social worker).

The Role of the Social Workers
The school employs a male and a female School Social Worker. Their roles include planning and implementing social programs for students struggling with social interactions amongst their peers and the teaching of life skills such as drug prevention, sexuality and the effects of alcohol.

The male School Social Worker is the senior of the two, although both provide individual counseling for the teachers, students and parents, and supports classroom teachers in class and accompanies students on field trips.

The senior School Social Worker plans and implements parent discussions and groups on current educational issues such as drinking alcohol, 'sexting' which involves sending nude images to others through a phone or internet website, and dealing with high pressure situations such as their final school examinations, aligned with the schools standards and expectations. The male School Social Worker is also responsible for arranging school holiday activities to keep students interested in their school life during their holiday breaks and increase their social skills, while the female School Social Worker assists the male coworker and attends the holiday activities to further support the students. The School Social Workers facilitate group study sessions for all students after school so they can keep up-to-date with their schoolwork and get extra support if needed, and encourages all students to get actively involved in the school's curricular sporting teams and school activities.

Collaboration between the School Social Workers and the classroom teachers occurs on a daily basis to ensure the wellbeing and best interests of the students. The one "inclusive" class at this school is made up of five students who are graded to be in Year 7, although their IQ levels are far below this standard. The teachers of this class have received additional training in inclusive practices, which ensures a consistency of practice across the school. The school does not employ any Teacher's Aides as the integration team believe that the stigma associated with helping students who may need their in-class support, will impact negatively on the student's self esteem and confidence (School Social Worker school D)

The male School Social Worker personally invites the migrant parents of students to come into the classrooms to feel "socially included" in the school environment, and arranges student payment for their role as translators for parents who struggle to understand German or English. One of the main barriers that exist between the School Social Worker and the students is the 'uncomfortableness' (School social worker school D) that sometimes occurs: some female students find it difficult to disclose personal information to a male, and therefore must wait until the female School Social Worker is present at the school. For students who are gifted, talented or gifted and talented, the School Social Workers can organise that they attend a university course during their schooling. These courses are offered to the students in their final years of schooling, for example if a student is excelling in computing studies and wishes to pursue this course, they are able to go to a university that has an alliance with the Gymnasium to accept these students. For students with intellectual disabilities, the School Social Worker tries to promote regular school attendance, and because of this they do not provide reports or grades for these students.The following table summarises key aspects of the *school D:*

3.9 Data Analysis

The data were analysed by identifying the common themes of the role of School Social Worker across the four different German schools. Of Friere's (1972) seven main concepts, this research drew from his concept of thematic analysis as he explains:

An epoch is characterized by a complex of ideas, concepts, hopes, doubts, values, and challenges in dialectical interaction with their opposites, striving towards plenitude. The concrete representation of many of these ideas, values, concepts, and hopes, as well as the obstacles which impede the people's full humanization, constitute the themes of that epoch. These themes imply others which are opposing or even antithetical; they also indicate tasks to be carried out and fulfilled. Thus, historical themes are never isolated, independent, disconnected, or static; they are always interacting dialectically with their opposites. Nor can these themes be found anywhere except in the human-world relationship. The complex of interacting themes of an epoch constitutes its "thematic universe." (Friere 1972, p.101).Interpretation of the themes found in the data were then applied to the NSW Education system as a comparison, and suggestions made as to what benefits the implementation of School Social workers in NSW schools could have.

3.9.1 Participant observation

Visual Ethnography research is intertwined with visual images and metaphors, and was used in this research as a form of observation as it involved "watching what happens and listening to what is said – asking questions" (Atkinson, 2005, p. 1 as cited in Pink, 2007, p. 22). The use of "visual ethnography" (Pink, 2007, p. 22) as a methodology is a concept that uses photography or images to support observations. According to Berg (2008, p. 935) the "visual representation provides a meaning for recording, documenting and explaining the social worlds and understandings of people", as well as adding a "visual medium" to the more common "verbal medium". Keegan (2008, p. 620) argued, "they complement the spoken word and often enable a richer, more holistic understanding of research participants' worlds".

The use of Visual Ethnography enabled the researcher to examine the roles and how the School Social Workers spent their time with students in class. The researcher was able to observe the School Social Worker use Therapy rooms, the layout of the classrooms and music and art rooms located within the school to support student learning within the Primary school system.

In line with the concept of Visual Ethnography, the researcher took a number of digital photographs of the schools that thereby helped in contextualising the interview and observational data from a visual perspective. As the research focus was on inclusive classroom practices, it was important to consider the classroom layout and settings in relation to the learning environment from the Teacher and School Social Workers' perspectives.

3.9.2 Summary

The observations, notes, photographs, interviews and discussions were useful to understand and comprehend the German Education System, and what role School Social Worker's played in the student's lives. In order to fully understand the important role of the School Social Worker in German Schools, it is relevant and essential that the German Education System be understood. Additionally, it is just as important that the Australian Education System, specifically in New South Wales be understood in order to accurately compare and analyse both Education systems.

3.10 Discussion

3.10.1 The German Education System:

The traditional German School System segregates their Secondary school students based on their academic ability and career aspirations post-school. After completing their Primary school years at the age of 10, students are required to choose which type of Secondary school they wish to attend. The 'Gymnasien' were designed for students who wish to prepare for a tertiary university education, and, students are offered a place at the Secondary school. This traditional structure of schooling may be viewed by some as being divisive, as schools may not accept all students that apply. This practice essentially works against the concept of inclusion. Since 2013, some 'Gymnasiums' such as the *school D* have begun enrolling students with disabilities and learning difficulties at their schools, and have adapted the learning content and outcomes to suit these individual students.

    The school D supports the concept of inclusion and the School Social Worker proudly stated, "enrolments for students with disabilities and learning difficulties had increased for the new 2014 academic year" (School social worker D). The School Social Worker explained how not all of the teachers in the school supported the implementation of 'inclusion', as teachers were so familiar with students performing at high levels that they felt underprepared on how to accommodate and differentiate tasks for students who may be achieving at a lower level, or those that presented with sound and/or vision impairments. The teachers also discussed at the school's regular weekly staff meeting that they often felt "judged" when support staff had to come into their classrooms to help individual students. Another issue for the school D was how they could realistically allocate their limited funding allocation from the Government to the incoming students presenting with special needs. For example, the School Social Worker explained how for one student, the school was required to purchase head sets with microphones for each student in the class so that the particular student with the hearing impairment would be able to hear their teacher and peers in all lessons adequately.

The four schools visited tended to adopt a range of learning orientations, one of which was the Montessori (Montessori, 2013) approach to learning, which "encourages independence by providing an environment of activities and materials which children can use at their own pace" (Montessori Australia, n.d). There are many positive features of the traditional German Education System, one being their differentiated curriculum and effective use of project-based learning. Project-based learning enables students to go through the process of inquiry in order to find a response to a question, problem or challenge. All teachers observed throughout the four German schools planned, managed and assessed their students' progress. They also helped them collaborate and communicate with their peers and the teacher to create high quality visual presentations.

Another strength of the German Education System was the active role the school-based Social Workers played in the student's lives. The School Social Workers at the schools were responsible for the following tasks:

- organising activities for the students in the school holidays and after-school;
- engaging in team-teaching with teachers;
- helping students develop friendship groups in and out of class;
- work on building student self-esteem and social skills;
- ensure correct information was communicated to parents from the school;
- conducting house visits to assess if the student's living conditions and home life were
- satisfactory;
- discuss with the parents the benefits of education for their children; and,
- advise them of financial and/or personal support services available to them. (School social Worker D).

All of the School Social Workers interviewed stated that they "were outside during recess and lunch" (School Social Worker B, C, D) to make themselves known to the students and encourage them to play together. All of the School Social Workers interviewed informed on how they were always available to the students. School Social Worker C (2013) stated that she was "always outside during recess and lunch" to make herself known to the students and encourage them to play actively with each other, and School Social Worker B (2013) stated, "I often sit in my office. Many people say the School Social Worker is always sitting in her office. In fact, everyday kids knock on my door, just to talk". School Social Worker D (2013) and Teacher school A (2013) were both observed during the day visiting the schools being available to the students during recess and lunch and having discussions with different groups of students.

The idea of financial hardship and divorce was very common for students in the areas of the schools visited, as these were all socio-economically disadvantaged areas with parents working extensive hours and minimal supervision for the children at home. The students brought many of their personal problems to school, which were constantly being addressed by the School Social Workers. School Social Worker B (2013) explained how "we are a deprived area here and the children bring a lot of massive problems to school", and some students at the school B have made confessions that "my mother is an alcoholic and I have been sexually abused". That excerpt was provided by the School Social Worker from a dialogue between them and two 8 year old girls. Moreover, School Social Workers run the "after school care" (School Social Worker school C) and "implementation of working groups in the afternoon sector" (School Social Worker school D).

The German Education System encouraged all parents to get involved in the learning of their children and to play an important role in the school community. Taeacher school A (2013) informed the researcher that "the parents of the students who attend the school have a fortnightly roster on what is required to be done around the school". The schools typically asked parents to volunteer time to clean the classrooms, support students with basic reading and mathematics similar to the role of a teacher's aide, attend school meetings with their children, and helping build equipment and set up rooms for student use. For example, at the school A relied on teachers and parents to set up specialist classrooms such as the art and music rooms, and clean their typical classrooms with tables and chairs and outdoor play area for the children. At the school B School Social Worker B (2013) explained how the "teachers do all of the maintenance and cleaning around the school" when they are also required to prepare their lessons and teach their classes.

The German Schools aim to include other family siblings that attended the school into each child's learning through the use of combined classes where students of various grades and ages were combined into the one class. The German Schools aimed to include other family siblings that attended the school into each child's learning through the use of combined classes where students of various grades and ages were combined into the one class. At the *school B* primary school, they "mix classes from the first to fourth grade" and have a maximum of "23 children in a class" (School Social Worker school B). Similarly, at the *Aktive Schule* primary school, they "combine grades one to three" (Teacher school A) and at the *school C*, they combine "grades one to three classes" (School Social Worker school C) . This blending of year levels was seen as being helpful for siblings to help teach the younger students the correct ways of the school, such as lining up before class and coming into the classroom, unpacking their belongings and removing their shoes prior to greeting the classroom teacher.

3.10.2 The NSW Education System:

The New South Wales Education system does not employ School Social Workers on staff in schools, but School Counselors. The School Counselors in NSW play a vital role in the development and mental state of many students, particularly those students with a disability or learning difficulty. As outlined earlier in this chapter, the School Counsellor role and responsibility in schools was defined by the NSW DEC as:
Provide counseling service to students;
- Work in consultation with other staff members to improve student learning and wellbeing;
- Carry out cognitive, social, emotional and behavioural assessments of students;
- Contribute to the development of and planning for students with special needs; and,
- refer students and their families onto the other agencies and support services that may be required to support health and wellbeing for the student and their families (NSW DEC, n.d, p. 3).

It seems evident that the NSW School Counselors do not play such an active, hands-on, prominent role with students when compared to the School Social Workers in Germany. The tasks both roles share include student counseling, intervention, teaching of social skills, and academic support for students. Both also provide information and additional support services for the student and their families if they lack access to resources and/or specialist skills to assist the student. Where the two roles differ markedly is the involvement with the student's home life: the NSW School Counselors are not permitted to have any contact with the students outside of school hours, nor visit the student's home and personally assess their home situation, unlike the German Social Workers are able to do.

There are a number of other differences between the roles and responsibilities of the German School Social Workers and the NSW School Counselors.

In the playground, the NSW School Counselors are not required to supervise students during playground duty during recess and lunchtime. In Germany, it is the responsibility of the Head Teacher of Welfare, and/or the Grade Year Advisors to organise activities for students that promote social skills and team activities. In the classroom, the NSW School Counsellor would not be present in the classroom, rather, it would be the responsibility of a Learning and Support Teacher to team-teach with the classroom teacher and then pass on any information deemed relevant to the School Counsellor. Any concerns the classroom teachers may have about a student are referred to the School Counsellor. Similarly in Germany, all students have the option of speaking to the School Social Worker when they have a problem about a situation occurring in or out of school.

An area of the New South Wales Education System of concern is that a great deal of responsibility, initiative and action is placed onto the parents of children with disabilities and learning difficulties, to ensure their child has access to the resources and supports they need to be fully included in the mainstream classroom. This puts a lot of pressure onto these parents as most would be unaware of what external services could support their child at school.

The new 2014 *National Curriculum for Australia* being implemented for Stages 4 and 5 in English, Mathematics, Science and History, is seen by many educators as a weakness in the NSW Educational System because although a National Curriculum means that all students in Australia will be taught the same content, it does not allow for differentiation to occur. The National curriculum is prescriptive in most areas and this does not encourage teachers to be innovative in their classrooms and use project-based learning on topics their students would find more interesting. The Australian Curriculum also does not explicitly inform teachers on the way that different and modern teaching methods should be put into practice. A concern of this is that some teachers who are not interested in embracing IT into their classes, would fail to incorporate Gardiner's (1983) *Multiple Intelligences framework* and *Bloom's Taxonomy* in their classes that cater for diversity. Gardiner (1983) argued that in order for a behavior to be considered an intelligence, it had to meet eight criteria, and these eight criteria manifest into eight abilities: i) musical–rhythmic; ii) visual–spatial; iii) verbal–linguistic; iv) logical–mathematical; v) bodily–kinesthetic; vi) interpersonal; vii) intrapersonal; and viii) naturalistic. He believed that all learners had their own unique blend of these abilities rather than identifying with just one ability. Translated into the classroom, educators are taught how to incorporate all of Gardiner's Multiple Intelligences in their teaching so as to make meaningful connections between their students and information. The NSW Education System should adapt to the German Education System where project-based learning and differentiation of curriculum is widely practiced. The project-based learning approach provides access to resources that cater for individual student needs that are guided by their teacher to participate in the inquiry process to achieve a result.

3.10.3 Future Recommendations

There are a number of recommendations based on the German Education system that the NSW Education department could consider incorporating into the daily policy and practices in their Primary and Secondary schools. One of the changes would involve re-visiting the role and involvement of parents and teachers in the school community to promote a whole-school collaborative student approach to learning at school. The German education system advocates for a more student-focused, student-driven education as supported by the Montessori school of thought. By allowing students the scope to explore their learning on their own terms, it is possible that teachers could incorporate a greater range of differentiated learning and teaching styles and pedagogies e.g. *Multiple Intelligences Framework* and *Bloom's Taxonomy*, into their curriculum. In doing so, the curriculum becomes more appealing and of interest to students, which in turn may promote higher levels of engagement and learning. Different teaching styles allows students to vary how they learn and select a learning style best suited to their needs that allows them to work at their own pace. Students engaged in more project-based and independent learning activities have the opportunity to have their learning needs expressed and their 'voice' heard, something that is often missed in traditional and conventional classrooms. This is an important point as the new Australian Curriculum being currently developed has a prescriptive focus on student achievement that has drawn criticism from educators as inhibiting student differentiation.

Differentiation of learning styles and preferences for student learning content was observed to work positively in the German Education System. Students did not need to be encouraged to complete their activities as they had chosen their own topics and learning areas they desired to learn about, and pursue across all of their main subject areas.

One suggestion based on this research that could be adapted into the New South Wales Education System, is the concept of students learning by 'doing', and teachers making learning more fun and enjoyable for students. Observations in the German Education System found that teachers couched student learning outcomes into game-like exploratory activities, so students were not explicitly told what they were learning, rather they were encouraged to use investigative strategies to solve problems. This teaching strategy allowed students to be engaged more effectively in their learning, and the classrooms reported less instances of classroom behavioural problems. Due to the successful nature of this strategy, the NSW Education System should consider integrating similar teaching strategies into their classrooms across all Primary and Secondary schools, in an effort to promote greater student engagement and experience less behavioural concerns in the classroom.

The German Education System needs to continue to work towards fostering and promoting inclusion in their school systems and further educate teachers and schools on the benefits of inclusion for all. A problem identified by the researcher in the German Schools was the segregation process of students into Secondary schools at the age of 10. Students who had a disability and/or a learning difficulty were previously not accepted into the Gymnasien. These students were not given a choice of which Gymnasium to attend based on their disability and/or learning difficulty. As of 2013, some Gymnasiums are now accepting all students regardless of student academic abilities which is an improvement from the older system, and may benefit future students. As such, the German Education System would need to ensure that not only should all students be given the option of attending the school of their choice, but that all schools provide a supportive school community that supports inclusion for all, and has access to enough funds to meet all the needs of these students and their teachers.

3.11 References

Ashman, A. F., Elkins J. (2012). Education for inclusion and diversity. Frenchs Forest, NSW Pearson
A
Australian Government Department of Health Services (2013) *Social Work Services.* Retrieved from
http://www.humanservices.gov.au/customer/services/centrelink/social-work-services
Australian Institute of Health and Welfare (2013) *Definition of Disability.* Retrieved from
https://www.aihw.gov.au/definition-of-disability/
Bloom, B.(Hrsg.) (1972). Taxonomie von Lernzielen im kognitiven Bereich. 4. Auflage. Beltz Verlag, Weinheim und Basel
Berg, B (2008) The SAGE Encyclopedia of Qualitative Research Methods. Given, L.
http://dx.doi.org.ezproxy.une.edu.au/10.4135/9781412963909
Cologon, K (2003). *Inclusion in Education: towards equality for students with disability.* Sydney, Australia: Children and Families Research Centre, Institute of Early Childhood Macquarie University
Dixon, R. M. and Verenikina, I. T. (2007). Towards Inclusive Schools: An Examination of Sociocultural Theory and Inclusive Practices and Policy in NSW DET Schools, *Learning and Socio-cultural Theory: Exploring Modern Vygotskian Perspectives International Workshop,* 1(1), 192-208. Retrieved from http://ro.uow.edu.au/cgi/viewcontent.cgi?article=1012&context=llrg
European Agency for Special Needs and Inclusive Education. (n.d). *Development of inclusion – Germany.* Retrieved from https://www.european-agency.org/country-information/germany/national-overview/development-of-inclusion
Evans, L (2007). *Inclusion.* Great Britain: Taylor and Francis.
Fan, M. (2004). *The idea of Integrated Education.* Georgia, United States of America: Valdosta State University.
Forbes, F. (2007). Inclusion Policy Towards Inclusion: an Australian Perspective. *Support for Learning.* 22(2), 66-71. Retrieved from http://www.waespaa.com.au/pdf/SupportForLearning-FionaForbes.pdf
Foreman, P. (2005). *Inclusion in action.* South Victoria, Australia: Thomson.

Friere, P. (1972) *Pedagogy of the Oppressed.* London: Penguin.

Gardiner, H. (1983). Frames of Mind: The Theory of Multiple Intelligences. London: Penguin.

Harman, B. (2002). *Inclusion/Integration: is there a difference?.* Retrieved from
http://www.cdss.ca/images/pdf/general_information/integration_vs_inclusion.pdf
International Classification of Functioning, Disability and Health. Retrieved from
http://www.who.int/classifications/icf/en/
James, A. (2010) *School Bullying.* Retrieved from http://www.nspcc.org.uk/inform/research/briefings/school_bullying_pdf_wdf73502.pdf
Jones, M, M. & McLean, K. J. (2012). Personalising Learning in Teacher Education through the use of Technology, *Australian Journal of Teacher Education,* 37 (1), 75-92. Retrieved from http://ro.ecu.edu.au/cgi/viewcontent.cgi?article=1604&context=ajte
Keegan, S. (2008). The SAGE Encyclopedia of Qualitative Research Methods. Given, L.
http://dx.doi.org.ezproxy.une.edu.au/10.4135/9781412963909.n318
Kerridge, G. (2008). *Learning Disability.* Retrieved from http://www.newcastle.edu.au/Resources/Divisions/Services/Student%20and%20Academic%20Services/Student%20Support/NDCO/NDCO_eZine_Aut08.pdf

Klemm, K. (2009). Effective Investment in Education, Exceptionalism Special Schools: a study on the issues and effectiveness of Special Schools in Germany. Gutersloh, Germany: Bertelsmann Foundation. Retrieved from http://translate.google.com/translate?depth=1&hl=en&prev=/search%3Fq%3Dinklusion%2Bin%2Bgerman%2Bschule%26biw%3D1243%26bih%3D609&rurl=translate.google.com.au&sl=de&u=http://www.bertelsmann-stiftung.de/cps/rde/xbcr/SID-CFD0B446-AC96034A/bst/Foerderschule.pdf

Klemm, K. (2012). *Information for Teachers and visiting Teachers, Inclusion: School for all shapes.* Bonn, Germany: Aktion Mensch eV. Retrieved from http://translate.google.com.au/translate?hl=en&sl=de&u=http://publikationen.aktion-mensch.de/unterricht/Aktion-Mensch_Inklusion_Praxisheft.pdf&prev=/search%3Fq%3DDefinition%2Bf%25C3%25BCr%2BInklusion%26biw%3D1245%26bih%3D595

Leavitt, M. (2006). Team Teaching: Benefits and Challenges, *Speaking of Teaching,* 16 (1), 1-4. Retrieved from http://www.stanford.edu/dept/CTL/Newsletter/teamteaching.pdf

Longhurst, R. (2010). *Semi-structured Interviews and Focus Groups.* Book is called: Key Methods in Geography. Nicholas Clifford, Shaun French & Gill Valentine. SAGE Publications.

Montessori Australia. (n.d) *Montessori Approach.* Retrieved from http://montessori.org.au/montessori/approach.htm

Montessori, M. (2013). *The Montessori Method.* New Jersey: Transaction Publishers.

McCrady, B. S., Ladd, B., Vermont, L. and Steele, J. (2010). *Interviews in Addiction Research Methods.* Oxford, UK: Wiley-Blackwell.

Nes, F.V., Abma, T., Jonsson, H. & Deeg, D. (2010). Language differences in qualitative research: is meaning lost in translation?, *European Journal of Ageing,* 7 (4), 313-316. Retrieved from http://www.ncbi.nlm.nih.gov/pmc/articles/PMC2995873/

NSW Board of Studies. (2002) .*K-10 Curriculum Framework.* Retrieved from http://www.boardofstudies.nsw.edu.au/manuals/pdf_doc/curriculum_fw_K10.pdf

NSW Department of Education and Communities. (n.d). *The School Counseling Workforce in NSW Government Schools.* Retrieved from https://www.det.nsw.edu.au/media/downloads/about-us/statistics-and-research/public-reviews-and-enquiries/school-counselling-services-review/paper1-tscwings.pdf

Opdenakker, R. (2006). Advantages and Disadvantages of Four Interview Techniques in Qualitative Research [44 paragraphs]. *Forum Qualitative Sozialforschung / Forum: Qualitative Social Research, 7*(4), Art. 11, http://nbn-resolving.de/urn:nbn:de:0114-fqs0604118.

Pink, S. (2007). *Doing Visual Ethnography.* London: SAGE Publications.

Roulston, K. (2012). *Reflective Interviewing: A Guide to Theory and Practice.* University of Georgia, USA: Sage Publications.

Rule, P. (2010). *Bakhtin and Friere: Dialogue, dialetic and boundary learning.* Educational Philosophy and Theory. DOI: 10.1111/j.1469-5812.2009.00606.x

Russ-Eft, D. & Preskill, H. (2009). Evaluation in Organizations: A Systematic Approach to Enhancing Learning, Performance, and Change. New York: Basic Books.

Urbis. (2011). Literature Review on Meeting: The Psychological and Emotional wellbeing needs of Children and Young People: Models of Effective Practice in Educational Settings. Retrieved from https://www.det.nsw.edu.au/media/downloads/about-us/statistics-and-research/public-reviews-and-enquiries/school-counselling-services-review/models-of-effective-practice.pdf

Hayley Matas und Ingrid Harrington
4 Die Rolle von Eltern, LehrerInnen und SozialarbeiterInnen im deutschen und australischen Bildungssystem

4.1 Zusammenfassung

Wer im australischen Bundesstaat New South Wales (NSW) als SchülerIn an einer staatlichen Grund- oder weiterführenden Schule angemeldet ist, hat ein Grundrecht auf Inklusion (Cologon, 2013, S.11). Dieses Kapitel liefert einen Vergleich der Bildungssysteme deutscher Grund- und weiterführender Schulen mit den entsprechenden Systemen in New South Wales unter besonderer Berücksichtigung der "Inklusionspraxis". Die Daten umfassen die inklusionsbezogenen Rollen und Sichtweisen von Eltern, LehrerInnen und SchulsozialarbeiterInnen an deutschen sowie BeratungslehrerInnen an australischen Schulen. Es wird versucht, die Bildungssysteme in NSW und Deutschland im Gesamtzusammenhang zu betrachten und signifikante Ergebnisse und Unterschiede herauszuarbeiten, die für die gegenwärtige Bildungspraxis in NSW relevant sein könnten.

4.2 Einleitung

An den öffentlichen und privaten Grund- und weiterführenden Schulen in Deutschland beziehungsweise Primary und Secondary Schools in Australien herrschen unterschiedliche Definitionen darüber, was 'Inklusion' im jeweiligen Bildungssetting bedeutet. Im Jahr 1997 schlugen alle australischen Schulen einen Weg der *full inclusion* ein, was bedeutete, dass alle SchülerInnen mit 'besonderen pädagogischen Bedürfnissen' "zusammen mit ihren AltersgenossInnen in Regelschulen unterrichtet werden sollten, um die Vorzüge der Inklusion zu verwirklichen" (Forbes 2007, S. 67). In den deutschen Bildungssettings bezieht sich 'Inklusion' auf 'offenere Formen des Lehrens und Lernens', um zu gewährleisten, dass alle SchülerInnen lernen und in der Klasse nicht benachteiligt werden (European Agency for Special Needs and Inclusive Education, o.J., S. 1). Neuere pädagogische Ansätze in Deutschland, die inkludierende Bildungspraktiken fördern, umfassen "das Lernen in heterogenen Gruppen, das Lehren mit unterschiedlichen Zielen, Wochenpläne, Learning by Doing und das Lernen mit allen Sinnen" (ebd.).

Inklusion
Die Begriffe 'Inklusion' und 'Integration' werden oft synonym verwendet, obwohl es wesentliche Unterschiede zwischen ihnen gibt. Nach Harman (2002, S. 1) steht bei der Inklusion im Vordergrund, jedes Kind innerhalb einer Regelklasse zu unterstützen; es geht darum, wie zusätzliche Hilfen und Anpassungen den Bedürfnissen aller Lernenden gerecht werden. Foreman (2005, S. 12) ist der Ansicht, dass Inklusion danach frage, *wie* den Bedürfnissen der Lernenden entsprochen werden kann. Je nach Art des besonderen Bedürfnisses müsse das Kind gegebenenfalls Spezialisten oder Beratungslehrer innerhalb oder außerhalb der Regelklasse aufsuchen. 'Integration' bezieht sich auf den Prozess, Kinder aus speziellen pädagogischen Settings in die Regelklasse zu führen, wo sie hauptsächlich, wenn nicht sogar vollständig unterrichtet werden sollen" (Ashman & Elkins 2012, S. 401). Für Foreman (2005, S. 12) fragt die Integration danach, '*ob* den Bedürfnissen der Lernenden entsprochen werden kann. Die Unterscheidung zwischen Inklusion und Integration ist von entscheidender Bedeutung, da es in der vorliegenden Untersuchung darum geht, ob eine von ihnen oder beide in deutschen Schulen zur Anwendung kommen.

Inklusion „führt zwar zur Integration" (Harman 2002, S. 1-2), reicht aber über die Erziehung hinaus und betrifft die Gesellschaft im Allgemeinen, in der Einzelne ungeachtet ihres kulturellen, ethnischen oder sozialen Hintergrunds akzeptiert werden.

In diesem Kapitel wollen wir unter inklusiver Praxis im Kontext des deutschen bzw. australischen Schulsystems verstehen:
- "das Erkennen verschiedener Arten von Begabungen und Fähigkeiten und die Schaffung von Erfolgsmöglichkeiten für alle" (Evans 2007, S. 6);
- die Rolle der Schule bei der Durchführung inklusiver Praktiken besteht darin, "eine Lernumgebung zu schaffen, in der Lernhindernisse, wo immer es möglich ist, vermieden werden" (Evans 2007, S. 6); und
- Integration in Schulen bedeutet, die einzelne Schülerin und den einzelnen Schüler als 'ganze' Person wahrzunehmen und zu gewährleisten, dass sie in ihre Schulumgebung und in ihr soziales Umfeld 'passt'.

Damit Integration und Inklusion gelingen können, ist es entscheidend, dass jede Person in der Schule Unterschiede anerkennt und andere ungeachtet ihrer jeweiligen Kultur, ihrer religiösen Überzeugung beziehungsweise ihrer Beeinträchtigungen respektiert (Fan, 2004). In diesem Beitrag wird diskutiert, was das Bildungssystem in NSW von dem in Deutschland lernen kann und welche Veränderungen am australischen System notwendig wären, um die Rollen von Eltern und SchulsozialarbeiterInnen im Schulalltag anzugleichen.

4.3 Literaturüberblick

4.3.1 Das Bildungssystem in NSW

Mit Beginn der 1980er Jahre legten die staatlichen Schulen in NSW ein größeres Augenmerk auf die geistige Gesundheit ihrer SchülerInnen. So gründete die Regierung 1999 eine *School-Link Initiative* (NSW DEC, o.J, S. 1), die es PädagogikstudentInnen an australischen Universitäten ermöglichte, Psychologiekurse zu belegen. Außerdem sollte die Schule als ganze darauf ausgerichtet sein, "die geistige Gesundheit von Kindern, Jugendlichen und jungen Erwachsenen in Schulen in NSW zu verbessern" (URBIS, 2011, S. 59 f.). Die *School-Link initiative* zielte darauf, psychische Probleme, die an Schulen auftreten können, zu erkennen und behandeln zu helfen und durch größeres Wissen, inner- und außerschulische Gemeinschaftsprojekte sowie die Entwicklung von Fähigkeiten und Fertigkeiten das Verständnis für Probleme der geistigen Gesundheit, mit denen junge Menschen konfrontiert werden, zu stärken.

In New South Wales bezieht sich der Ausdruck 'SchülerInnen mit einer Behinderung (*disability*) oder zusätzlichen Lernbedürfnissen' (NSW DEC, 2013) auf Lernende, die "möglicherweise irgendwann in ihrer Schullaufbahn aufgrund einer behindernden Bedingung zusätzliche Hilfe benötigen" (URBIS, 2011, S. 50). Es ist wichtig festzuhalten, dass die Kategorien Lern*behinderung* (*learning disability*) und Lern*schwierigkeit* (*learning difficulty*) in derselben Richtlinie des Department of Education and Communities (DEC) abgehandelt werden, obwohl sie sich wesentlich unterscheiden. Eine *Behinderung* ist definiert als "mindestens eine von 17 Einschränkungen, Beeinträchtigungen oder Schädigungen, von denen angenommen werden kann, dass sie für einen Zeitraum von mindestens sechs Monaten andauern und eine Person in ihren täglichen Aktivitäten einschränken" (Australian Institute of Health and Welfare 2013, S. 1).

Im 1992 vom australischen Staat verabschiedeten *Disability Discrimination Act* wird Lernbehinderung definiert als eine "Störung oder Dysfunktion, die dazu führt, dass jemand anders lernt als jemand, der die Störung oder Dysfunktion nicht aufweist" (Kerridge 2008, S. 1).

Entscheidend ist bei diesen beiden Definitionen, dass sie von der Prämisse ausgehen, dass eine Lern*schwierigkeit* mit den richtigen Unterstützungen, geeignetem Personal und genügend Zeit verbessert werden kann, während die Diagnose einer Lern*behinderung* sich eher nicht mehr ändert, auch wenn sich ihre Symptome und Merkmale verbessern lassen. Im Ergebnis hat die Inklusionsrichtlinie des DEC dazu geführt, dass SchülerInnen mit Lernbehinderungen bzw. -schwierigkeiten an Regelschulen und in Regelklassen aufgenommen werden können. Angesichts der Zahl der SchülerInnen, die den oben genannten Kriterien einer

Lernschwierigkeit oder -behinderung entsprachen, erhöhte das Department of Education and Communities von New South Wales seine Ausgaben in staatlichen Schulen zwischen 2009 und 2011 um 76 Prozent (URBIS 2011, S. 50). Das New South Wales Board of Studies (NSW BOS), das die Richtlinien der LehrerInnenausbildung bestimmt, legt in Anerkennung der neuen Inklusionsvorgaben fest:
(a) Alle SchülerInnen müssen die Möglichkeit haben, selbst zu lernen, für ihr Lernen verantwortlich zu sein und ihr Lernen fortzusetzen;
(b) alle SchülerInnen haben Anspruch auf die Aneignung von Wissen, Fähigkeiten, Verständnis und Werten;
(c) Bildung muss alle SchülerInnen, die eine Schule in NSW besuchen, mit einschließen;
(d) LehrerInnen, Schulen und Schulbehörden entscheiden darüber, wie das Lernen der SchülerInnen maximiert werden soll (NSW Board of Studies: K-10 Curriculum Framework, 2002)

Im Lichte der Richtlinien der Disability Standards for Education (2005) und des Disability Discrimination Act (1992) haben sich die pädagogischen Möglichkeiten für LehrerInnen erhöht. In Anerkennung dieser wichtigen Dokumente führte das DEC unter dem Titel Special Education Initiative 2006-2007 ein Programm ein, das zum Ziel hatte, den Herausforderungen der besonderen Bedürfnisse der SchülerInnen an allen staatlichen Primary und Secondary Schools in NSW gerecht zu werden. Die Disability Standards for Education (2005) und der Disability Discrimination Act (1992) führten dazu, dass Eltern in New South Wales ihre Kinder zum ersten Mal an einer Schule ihrer Wahl anmelden konnten (Dixon & Verenikina, 2007). Die Unterstützung, die SchülerInnen mit Behinderungen bzw. Lernschwierigkeiten in Regelklassen zuteilwurde, variierte je nach Art ihrer Bedürfnisse und je nachdem, was die Schule zu leisten imstande war. In den meisten Fällen wurden SchülerInnen mit besonderen Lernbedürfnissen in Regelklassen mit RegelschülerInnen unterrichtet und einzeln oder gemeinsam mit anderen von UnterrichtsassistentInnen unterstützt. Bei anderen SchülerInnen waren die lernbezogenen oder sozialen Bedürfnisse so groß, dass sie innerhalb der Struktur der Regelschule mit gleichartigen SchülerInnen in einer Förderklasse unterrichtet wurden, gleichzeitig aber auch am Regelunterricht teilnahmen, wobei sie in bestimmten Fächern zusätzliche Unterstützung erhielten. Mittlerweile wird von allen LehrerInnen in NSW erwartet, dass sie SchülerInnen mit Lernbehinderungen bzw. -schwierigkeiten in ihrer Regelklasse unterrichten. Diverse Veränderungen auf der Landes- und Bundesregierungsebene führten dazu, dass die Finanzierung von UnterrichtsassistentInnen und BetreuungslehrerInnen einer genauen Prüfung unterzogen wurde. Die Förderanträge, die Schulleiter, Eltern oder UnterrichtsassistentInnen zu stellen hatten, um Hilfen für einzelne SchülerInnen zu erhalten, wurden komplexer und anspruchsvoller und der Förderbedarf musste sehr ausführlich begründet werden. Die Folge war, dass der Bedarf an Förderung durch UnterrichtsassistentInnen in den Regelklassen stieg, die Zahl der UnterrichtsassistentInnen aber abnahm oder stagnierte. Zur Veranschaulichung: Vor fünf Jahren wären in einer Regelklasse mit zwei SchülerInnen mit einer Behinderung und fünf SchülerInnen mit Förderbedarf aufgrund von Lernschwierigkeiten zwei UnterrichtsassistentInnen im Einsatz gewesen, die diese Kinder bis zu sechs Stunden täglich in Vollzeit betreut hätten. Heute dagegen gäbe es für dieselben sieben SchülerInnen nur noch eine Hilfskraft, die den Kindern für zwei Stunden am Tag eine gemeinschaftliche Förderung bieten könnte

Die Schulen in NSW können BeratungslehrerInnen in Anspruch nehmen, die mit SchülerInnen, Eltern und Lehrkräften arbeiten, um professionelle Hilfen und Einschätzungen von SchülerInnen mit speziellen Bedürfnissen anzubieten. Um als BeratungslehrerIn eingestellt werden zu können, muss man einen pädagogischen Abschluss vorweisen und eine Zusatzausbildung machen. Die BeratungslehrerInnen an Schulen in NSW haben die Aufgabe, SchülerInnen zu beraten, in Absprache mit den anderen MitarbeiterInnen der Schule das Lernen und das Wohlbefinden der SchülerInnen zu fördern, kognitive, soziale und verhaltensbezogene Beurteilungen abzugeben, sich an der Entwicklung und Planung für SchülerInnen mit besonderen Bedürfnissen zu beteiligen und SchülerInnen und deren Familien an andere zur Förderung der Gesundheit und des Wohlbefindens der SchülerInnen und ihrer Familien notwendige Stellen und Unterstützungseinrichtungen zu vermitteln(NSW DEC, o.J., S. 3).

Aus ökonomischen Rationalisierungsgründen kann es vorkommen, dass sich sechs bis acht Schulen in einer Region eine Beratungslehrkraft teilen, oder anders ausgedrückt, dass eine Beratungslehrkraft nur höchstens einmal pro Woche an einer Schule tätig ist. Ihre Arbeit ist also naturgemäß stark gefragt und sehr kurzfristig, da kaum eine Schule über eigene BeratungslehrerInnen verfügt. Die BeratungslehrerInnen arbeiten an Grund- und weiterführenden Schulen mit SchülerInnen von der Vorschule bis zum zwölften Schuljahr (NSW DEC, 2013).

Das Bildungssystem in NSW reicht vom Kindergarten bis zum zwölften Schuljahr ('K-12'). Der primäre Bildungsbereich (*Primary School*) beginnt mit dem Kindergarten und endet mit dem sechsten Schuljahr, wobei diese sieben Jahre in drei 'Stufen' unterteilt sind: Das Kindergartenjahr und die ersten beiden Schuljahre entsprechen Stufe 1, das dritte und vierte Schuljahr Stufe 2 und das fünfte und sechste Schuljahr Stufe 3. Das Stufenmodell bietet den LehrerInnen die Möglichkeit, die Lehrpläne flexibel an ein größeres Fähigkeits- und Altersspektrum anzupassen, daher gibt es 'gemischte' Klassen, die sich beispielsweise aus SchülerInnen des ersten und zweiten oder des fünften und sechsten Schuljahrs zusammensetzen. Nach Abschluss der Grundschule führen die SchülerInnen ihre Ausbildung im sekundären Bildungsbereich (siebtes bis zwölftes Schuljahr) weiter. Das Stufenmodell setzt sich auch hier fort (7. und 8. Schuljahr = Stufe 4; 9. und

10. Schuljahr = Stufe 5; 11. und 12. Schuljahr = Stufe 6). Anders als im deutschen Bildungssystem findet keine formelle Selektion nach der voraussichtlichen Berufswahl der SchülerInnen statt. Alle SchülerInnen haben nach Vollendung des zehnten Schuljahrs die Möglichkeit, die Schule mit einem '*Year 10 Certificate*' zu verlassen und andere Lernwege einzuschlagen, zum Beispiel Berufsakademien (*Technical and Further Education*, TAFE), Lehrstellen usw. Wer das zwölfte Schuljahr vollendet, erreicht das sogenannte *Higher School Certificate* (HSC) und wird anhand eines Punktesystems (*Australian Tertiary Admission Rank*, ATAR) bewertet, das entscheidend für den Zugang zu tertiären Bildungseinrichtungen und Universitäten ist. Wer beispielsweise Veterinärmedizin studieren möchte, braucht eine ATAR-Punktzahl von über 93 Prozent, für ein Pädagogikstudium reichen 71 Prozent. Eine Politik der Deregulierung und die Verringerung der Studienplatzförderung seitens der Regierung haben mittlerweile dazu geführt, dass die Universitäten als eigenständige Unternehmen fungieren müssen, die wirtschaftlich darauf angewiesen sind, Studierende anzulocken und zu halten. In der Realität wird der Konkurrenzdruck für SchülerInnen jedoch größer, weil die Universitäten Bewerber mit höheren ATAR-Punktzahlen bevorzugen. Das führt zum Beispiel dazu, dass jemand, der ein Pädagogikstudium anstrebt und auch die nötigen 71 Prozent erreicht hat, trotzdem keinen Studienplatz bekommt, weil sich die Hochschule aufgrund der Konkurrenzsituation erlauben kann, Studienplätze erst ab einer ATAR-Punktzahl von 80 Prozent zu vergeben. In den 1980er Jahren war die tertiäre Bildung kostenlos, heute dagegen ist ein Hochschulstudium aufgrund der Maßnahmen der Regierung teuer, denn die Studierenden müssen pro Kurs und pro Semester bezahlen. Auch hier variieren die Studiengebühren wieder je nach Studienfach; so kostet etwa ein Kurs in Veterinärmedizin durchschnittlich 3.500 bis 5.000 AUD, während sich ein Kurs in Pädagogik auf etwa 700 bis 850 AUD beläuft.

Im Allgemeinen können Eltern und SchülerInnen die weiterführende Schule frei wählen, sei sie staatlich oder privat. Um Eltern besser darüber zu informieren, welche akademischen, sozialen, sportlichen, berufsvorbereitenden oder kreativen Bildungsinhalte eine Schule anbietet, hat das NSW DEC eine Internetseite mit dem Namen *My School* eingerichtet. Auf dieser Seite können Eltern herausfinden und bewerten, welche Schule am besten zu den Fähigkeiten und Berufsvorstellungen ihrer Kinder 'passt'. Sie stellt vergleichende Diagramme und Statistiken über die akademischen, sozialen, sportlichen, berufsbezogenen und kreativen Bildungsinhalte der einzelnen Schulen zur Verfügung. Schon bald nach dem Start der Website wurde deutlich, dass die Anmeldezahlen an einigen staatlichen Schulen in die Höhe schnellten – auf Kosten anderer, die im Ranking nicht so gut abschnitten. Um dem entgegenzusteuern, machte das DEC die Berechtigung zur Anmeldung an einer bestimmten weiterführenden Schule in stärkerem Maße vom jeweiligen Wohnort der SchülerInnen abhängig. Außer in Ausnahmefällen wurden Eltern damit verpflichtet, ihre Kinder an die entsprechende Schule in ihrer

Region zu schicken. Wenn diese Schule den Eltern aus irgendwelchen Gründen inakzeptabel erschien, war es eine gängige Praxis, in die gewünschte Gegend umzuziehen oder sein Kind an einer privaten Schule anzumelden. Privatschulen sind in Australien teuer – die jährliche Schulgebühr beträgt etwa 8.000 bis 10.000 AUD für Grundschulen und 20.000 bis 35.000 AUD für weiterführende Schulen. Da diese Summen für eine Durchschnittsfamilie unbezahlbar sind, stehen die staatlichen Schulen unter immensem Druck, allen SchülerInnen eine exzellente Bildung zu ermöglichen.

4.3.2 Das deutsche Bildungssystem

Das deutsche Bildungssystem stellt sich in den einzelnen Regionen unterschiedlich dar, da jedes Bundesland eigenständig über seine Bildungspolitik bestimmen kann. Die meisten Kinder besuchen vom sechsten bis zum zehnten Lebensjahr die Grundschule, die der australischen *Primary School* entspricht. Danach werden sie entsprechend ihrer berufsbezogenen bzw. akademischen Fähigkeiten einer weiterführenden Schule zugeteilt.
Die drei Hauptarten von weiterführenden Schulen sind:
1) *Gymnasium* – soll SchülerInnen auf die tertiäre universitäre Ausbildung vorbereiten; wird nach der zwölften Klasse mit dem Abitur abgeschlossen.
2) *Realschule* – zielt auf die Vermittlung einer erweiterten Grundbildung; den Abschluss bildet die sogenannte 'Mittlere Reife' nach der zehnten Klasse.
3) *Hauptschule* – die am wenigsten akademische Schulform; soll die SchülerInnen auf ihren späteren Beruf vorbereiten; endet nach einer Prüfung in der neunten oder zehnten Klasse mit dem Hauptschulabschluss.
Bis vor weniger als fünf Jahren wurden in Deutschland SchülerInnen mit besonderen Bedürfnissen noch nicht in Regelschulen unterrichtet. Kinder, bei denen Lernschwierigkeiten bzw. eine Lernbehinderung diagnostiziert wurde, besuchten spezielle Schulen, die sogenannten 'Förderschulen' oder 'Sonderschulen'. Als die Idee der 'inklusiven Pädagogik' weltweit an immer mehr Schulen in die Praxis umgesetzt wurde, gerieten die *Förder-* und *Sonderschulen* stark in die Kritik, weil sie SchülerInnen mit einer Behinderung oder Lernschwierigkeiten diskriminierten und von den Regelschulklassen absonderten. In meiner Datensammlung fand ich interessanterweise eine kleine Zahl von SchülerInnen, bei denen eine Behinderung bzw. Lernschwierigkeit festgestellt worden war und die in Hauptschulen und Gymnasien integriert waren. Das Umdenken, das dazu führte, dass SchülerInnen mit Behinderungen oder Lernschwierigkeiten nicht mehr in Sonderschulen, sondern in Regelklassen unterrichtet werden sollten, hatte allerdings Optionseinbußen für die betroffenen Eltern zur Folge, insbesondere einen Verlust finanzieller Unterstützungsleistungen durch den Staat. Aus diesem Grund wurde die Überführung

von SchülerInnen mit speziellen Bedürfnissen in die Regelklasse sehr sorgfältig organisiert, um niemanden zu benachteiligen.

Die Idee der 'Inklusion' an deutschen Schulen lässt sich am besten wiedergeben als eine Haltung, "die jedes Kind in seiner Individualität wertschätzt und Vielfalt als Bereicherung für erfolgreiches Lernen aller Schülerinnen und Schüler erkennt" (Aktion Mensch 2012, S.4).

Eltern, LehrerInnen und SchulsozialarbeiterInnen, die die Idee der Inklusion befürworten, sind davon überzeugt, dass es nicht nötig ist, SchülerInnen mit Behinderungen oder Lernschwierigkeiten in Gruppen zu isolieren und abzusondern; sie vertreten vielmehr die Ansicht, dass die Bedürfnisse aller SchülerInnen in der Regelklasse erfüllt werden können. Deutsche Schulen, die eine inklusive Lernumgebung unterstützen, berichten, dass SchülerInnen ohne spezielle Bedürfnisse vom gemeinsamen Lernen mit SchülerInnen mit speziellen Bedürfnissen in ihrer Klasse profitieren, weil "soziale Kompetenzen und gegenseitiger Respekt gefördert werden" (Aktion Mensch, 2012, S. 3).

An deutschen Schulen gibt es keine Schuluniformen oder einheitliche Bekleidungsvorschriften. Ein Argument, das häufig im Zusammenhang mit Schuluniformen vorgebracht wird, ist, dass es durch die freie Kleiderwahl eher zu Mobbing unter den SchülerInnen kommen könne, da sie einander nach der Auswahl und 'Angesagtheit' ihrer Kleidung beurteilten. Ich habe diese Praxis während meiner Datenerhebung weder beobachtet noch wurde mir von den befragten Schulbediensteten berichtet, dass dies ein aktuelles Thema oder Problem sei.

4.3.3   Vergleich des deutschen und des australischen Bildungssystems

Die Untersuchung der Bildungssysteme in Deutschland und New South Wales, Australien, macht evident, dass es zwischen der deutschen und der australischen Schulpraxis Gemeinsamkeiten und Unterschiede gibt.
Zu den Unterschieden gehören:

Deutsches Bildungssystem	Australisches Bildungssystem
Einteilung der SchülerInnen nach ihren *akademischen Fähigkeiten*	Einteilung der SchülerInnen nach ihren *besonderen Bedürfnissen*
SchulsozialarbeiterInnen gehören zum festen Personal einer Schule; sie sind stärker in die sozialen und familiären Probleme der SchülerInnen ein-	*BeratungslehrerInnen* sind auf mehrere Schulen aufgeteilt und kümmern sich formell nicht um die außerschulische Umgebung. Ihre Tätigkeit beschränkt sich auf die Unterstützung

bezogen, können diese auch außerhalb der Schulzeit kontaktieren und Hausbesuche veranlassen.	der SchülerInnen mit rein innerschulischen Mitteln und innerhalb der Schulzeit.
Eltern und LehrerInnen entscheiden gemeinsam über bestimmte schulische Ereignisse für alle SchülerInnen.	Eltern und LehrerInnen treffen eventuell gemeinsam Entscheidungen für einzelne SchülerInnen, aber nicht für die ganze Klasse.

Tabelle 4-1 Unterschiede zwishcen dem deutschen und australischen Bildungssystem

Zu den Gemeinsamkeiten gehören:

Deutsches Bildungssystem	Australisches Bildungssystem
Getrennte primäre (Grundschule: 6. bis 10. Jebensjahr) und sekundäre (Gymnasium, Realschule, Hauptschule: 11. bis 18. Lebensjahr) Schulstufen.	Getrennte primäre ((Kindergarten bis 6. Klasse) und sekundäre (7. bis 12. Klasse) Schulstufen.
SchulsozialarbeiterInnen bieten unterstützende Dienste wie Beratung, Intervention und akademische Hilfe für die SchülerInnen an.	*BeratungslehrerInnen* bieten unterstützende Dienste wie Beratung, Intervention und akademische Hilfe für die SchülerInnen an.
Es gibt einen *Hauptschulabschluss* nach dem 10. Schuljahr, mit dem SchülerInnen eine Berufsausbildung beginnen können.	Es gibt das *TAFE*-System nach dem 10. Schuljahr, mit dem SchülerInnen eine Berufsausbildung beginnen können.

Tabelle 4-2 Gemeinsamkeiten zwischen dem deutschen und australischen Bildungssystem

Der Hauptunterschied zwischen den beiden Systemen scheint zu sein, dass SchulsozialarbeiterInnen in Deutschland fest an einer Schule beschäftigt sind, während sich in Australien mehrere Schulen einen Beratungslehrer oder eine Beratungslehrerin teilen müssen. Ihre Rollen sind dabei jeweils klar definiert. Die Aufgabe von SchulsozialarbeiterInnen in Australien besteht laut Australian Government Department of Health Services (2013, S. 1) darin, "in Form von kurzfristiger Beratung, Erkundung von Möglichkeiten und Bereitstellung von Informationen zu helfen und zu unterstützen", was für SchulsozialarbeiterInnen an deutschen Schulen ebenso gilt. Die Definition ist also in beiden Ländern gleich, aber nur Deutschland stellt SchulsozialarbeiterInnen an Schulen ein.

4.4 Methodik

Die Untersuchung wurde von einer ausgebildeten australischen Grundschullehrerin geleitet, die als 'Beginning Teacher' tätig war, wie man in Australien LehrerInnen in den ersten fünf Jahren nach dem Examen nennt. Sie arbeitete mit einer Gruppe von drei Studierenden der Sozialen Arbeit der Fachhochschule Dortmund zusammen. Gemeinsam besuchten sie vier deutsche Schulen, beobachteten den Schulalltag und führten Interviews mit MitarbeiterInnen, insbesondere LehrerInnen und SchulsozialarbeiterInnen.

Der Fokus der Untersuchung lag auf drei Grundschulen und einer weiterführenden Schule. Einer der Hauptgründe für die Wahl dieser Schulen war, dass sie SchülerInnen mit Behinderungen oder Lernschwierigkeiten in ihren Regelklassen aufnahmen. Wegen der mangelnden deutschen Sprachkenntnisse des australischen Forschungsmitglieds traf sich die Arbeitsgruppe am Ende jeder Datenerhebungsrunde, um zu diskutieren und auszutauschen, was sie über die besuchten Schulen jeweils in Erfahrung gebracht hatte. Aufgrund des begrenzten Zeitrahmens von zwei Wochen, der für die Datensammlung aus den Schulen zur Verfügung stand, wurde darüber hinaus beschlossen, nur bestimmte Datenerhebungsmethoden zu nutzen, nämlich Klassenraumbeobachtungen, halbstrukturierte und informelle Interviews.

Zum Schutz der Privatsphäre der SchülerInnen wurden dem Forschungsteam keine Namen genannt und es durften keine direkten Fotos gemacht werden.

Die halbstrukturierten Interviews ermöglichten es, die Fragen im Sinne der Forschungsarbeit zu formulieren, während die offenen Fragen anschaulichere Antworten zuließen (Opdenakker, 2006, S.1). Auch die Technik der Klassenraumbeobachtung wurde genutzt, da sie einfach und schnell umzusetzen war und einen lebendigen 'Schnappschuss' eines typischen Schultags bot. Es war wichtig, dafür zu sorgen, dass die Beobachtenden, d.h. das Forschungsteam, möglichst unsichtbar blieben, um zu gewährleisten, dass sich die SchülerInnen möglichst normal verhielten (Russ-Eft & Preskill, 2009).

Klassenraumbeobachtung

Der Großteil der Daten wurde durch Beobachtungen der SchülerInnen in ihren Regelklassen gesammelt. Dabei wurden Notizen über das Verhalten der SchülerInnen, ihre Einstellung zum Lernen sowie ihre Fähigkeit, Arbeiten in einer schülerorientierten Lernumgebung selbständig abzuschließen, gemacht. Die Variablen, die für die verschiedenen Beobachtungen herangezogen wurden, umfassten a) Zeitpunkt der Beobachtung, b) Geschlecht, c) Aufgabenstellung, d) Schulfach, e) Fähigkeiten der Schülerin/des Schülers laut Angaben der Klassenlehrerin/des Klassenlehrers und f) Störungen im Klassenraum.

Die meisten beobachteten Schulstunden waren Englischunterricht in englischer Sprache. Das ermöglichte es dem australischen Forschungsmitglied, dem Unterrichtsinhalt zu folgen. Es ging um das Erlernen des englischen Alphabets sowie das Stellen und Beantworten einfacher Fragen auf Englisch.
Notiert wurde die Mitarbeit der SchülerInnen in der Klasse und ihre Reaktionen auf Anweisungen des Lehrers oder der Lehrererin. Dies war grundlegend für die Untersuchung, denn um die Rolle der Sozialarbeiters/der Sozialarbeiterin im Schulalltag einschätzen zu können, war es wesentlich, zu verstehen, welche Lernvorlieben die SchülerInnen hatten und wie sie in der Klasse mitarbeiteten. Die Beobachtungen wurden von einer Reihe von Fragen über das deutsche Schulsystem geleitet:

- Waren die SchülerInnen immer bei der Sache? Wann waren sie nicht bei der Sache?
- Wählten die SchülerInnen ihre Aufgaben in einem Schwierigkeitsgrad, der sie angemessen forderte?
- Beschäftigten sich die Kinder beim Lernen aktiv mit ihren MitschülerInnen oder arbeiteten sie ausschließlich für sich?
- Welche Mittel und Wege zum selbstbestimmten Lernen gaben die Lehrkräfte den SchülerInnen an die Hand?
- Wirkten die SchülerInnnen zufrieden mit ihrer Arbeit?

Anmerkung: Der Zweck dieser Frage lag darin, einzuschätzen, ob die SchülerInnen mit ihren Arbeitsergebnissen zufrieden waren. Da der Großteil der Arbeit schülerorientiert war, war es wichtig festzustellen, ob die Kinder ihre Aufgaben hastig erledigten, um gute Beurteilungen zu bekommen oder Lob zu ernten, oder ob sie alles daran setzten, ihre Aufgaben nach besten Kräften fertigzustellen.Gab es irgendwelche Probleme dadurch, dass es SchülerInnen mit besonderen Bedürfnissen in der Klasse gab? Wenn ja, welche? Wie wurde darauf eingegangen? Des Weiteren wurde beobachtet, wie die SchulsozialarbeiterInnen außerhalb der offiziellen Schulstunden mit den SchülerInnen interagierten, beispielsweise während das Forschungsteam in der Pause und zum Mittagessen über das Schulgelände geführt wurde. Die Beobachtung der Interaktion und der Körpersprache der SchülerInnen machte deutlich, dass sie den SchulsozialarbeiterInnen ein hohes Maß an Respekt entgegenbrachten und sich bei ihnen ausnahmslos wohlfühlten.

4.4.1 Halbstrukturierte, informelle Interviews

Informelle, halbstrukturierte Interviews wurden durchgeführt, weil sie direkte Antworten auf die vom Forschungsteam gestellten Fragen lieferten, aber auch

Spielräume zuließen (Roulston, 2012, S.12). Nach Longhurst (2010, S. 103) ist ein halbstrukturiertes Interview "ein verbaler Austausch, bei dem eine Person, der Interviewer/die Interviewerin, versucht, einer anderen Person Informationen zu entlocken, indem sie Fragen stellt". Eine der Stärken dieser Art von Interviews liegt darin, dass sie "den Teilnehmenden die Möglichkeit [bieten], Fragen zu erörtern, die sie für wichtig halten" (Longhurst, 2010, S. 103). Die Semistrukturiertheit der Interviews ließ den SchulsozialarbeiterInnen auch 'Raum', um auf Fragen näher einzugehen. Die Ergebnisoffenheit der Fragen erlaubt es laut Roulston (2012, S. 12) "den Befragten, Antworten auf vom Interviewer oder der Interviewerin vorgegebene Themen in eigenen Worten zu formulieren".

Aus organisatorischen Gründen – etwa der Beschaffung von Interviewgenehmigungen für SchülerInnen oder Terminbeschränkungen bei Schulen und SchulsozialarbeiterInnen – wurden während des Forschungsprojekts nur SchulsozialarbeiterInnen und Lehrkräfte und keine SchülerInnen befragt. Die Interviews dauerten ungefähr eine Stunde und wurden aufgezeichnet sowie vollständig auf Englisch transkribiert. Sie fanden während der Schulzeit im Büro der SchulsozialarbeiterInnen oder im LehrerInnenzimmer statt.

Für die SchulsozialarbeiterInnen an den Grund- und weiterführenden Schulen wurde folgende Liste mit halbstrukturierten Fragen verwendet: Beschreiben Sie, was Ihre Rolle als SozialarbeiterIn an dieser Schule beinhaltet und was sie zur Unterstützung von SchülerInnen und LehrerInnen beiträgt.
1) Wie oft treffen Sie sich mit dem Klassenlehrer/der Klassenlehrerin, um SchülerInnenangelegenheiten zu besprechen? Um welche Fragen geht es bei diesen Gesprächen üblicherweise?
2) Welche Unterstützung bieten Sie den KlassenlehrerInnen für ihren Unterricht? Glauben Sie, dass es SchülerInnen gibt, die auf Sie besser reagieren als auf ihre KlassenlehrerIn? Woran liegt das Ihrer Meinung nach? Beschreiben Sie diese Art von SchülerInnen.
3) Beschreiben Sie einige der beliebtesten und erfolgreichsten Strategien, die Sie bei der Arbeit mit SchülerInnen in der Klasse eingesetzt haben. Welche Strategien würden Sie anderen LehrerInnen zur Anwendung in inklusiven Klassen empfehlen? Richten sich Ihre Strategien auf bestimmte kleine Veränderungen im Alltag eines Schülers/einer Schülerin oder geht es ihnen eher um eine breitere Wirkung, die die Schule als ganze umfasst?
4) Welche Arten von SchülerInnen mit speziellen Bedürfnissen gibt es in Ihrer Klasse? Wie viele SchülerInnen mit Behinderung haben Sie in Ihrer Klasse im Vergleich zu SchülerInnen mit Lernschwierigkeiten?
5) Welche Strategien setzen Sie ein, um auf individuelle Bedürfnisse von SchülerInnen einzugehen? Gelten diese für SchülerInnen mit oder ohne Behinderung/Lernschwierigkeiten?

6) Wie ermutigen und fördern Sie als SozialarbeiterIn qualifiziertes Engagement und Beteiligung unter den SchülerInnen?
7) Welche Dinge besprechen die SchülerInnen mit Ihnen? Wie hilft Ihnen dies dabei, die SchülerInnen in der Klasse zu unterstützen?
8) Welche Art von Ausbildung ist am ehesten notwendig, um das Schulpersonal auf die Arbeit mit SchülerInnen mit besonderen Bedürfnissen und ihre individuellen Voraussetzungen vorzubereiten? Erörtern Sie einige erfolgreiche Ausbildungsbeispiele.

Der Austausch mit den anderen, am Forschungsprojekt beteiligten, bot uns die Möglichkeit, unsere verschiedenen Beobachtungen an den jeweiligen Schulen zu vergleichen, etwa in Bezug darauf, wie sie auf SchülerInnen mit Behinderungen/Lernschwierigkeiten eingingen, welche Dienstleistungen den SchülerInnen in der Schule zur Verfügung standen oder welche Pädagogik die LehrerInnen zur Umsetzung des Lehrplans wählten. Da das australische Forschungsmitglied Deutsch weder verstand noch sprach, waren Übersetzungsleistungen notwendig, um eine Verständigung unter allen Beteiligten möglich zu machen. Van Nes, Abma, Jonsson und Deeg (2010, S. 313) erklären, dass "die Sprache [...] in allen Phasen zentral [ist], von der Datenerhebung bis zur Analyse und Darstellung". Die aus drei Deutschen und einer Australierin bestehende Forschungsgruppe traf sich am Ende jedes Schulbesuchs für eine Stunde, um die Datenerhebung des Tages zu diskutieren. Diese Nachbesprechungen waren äußerst wertvoll, denn sie gewährleisteten, dass alle Mitglieder informiert und auf dem neuesten Stand waren. Dieses Vorgehen verringerte die Wahrscheinlichkeit einer Fehlinterpretation oder Falschdarstellung der Daten.

4.4.2 Auswahl der Schulen

Für die Untersuchung wurden vier Schulen ausgewählt, die mit einem Forschungsprojekt zur inklusiven Pädagogik der Fachhochschule Dortmund verbunden waren, über festangestellte SchulsozialarbeiterInnen verfügten und eine Reihe von inklusiven Strategien anwendeten, um den Bedürfnissen ihrer SchülerInnen gerecht zu werden. Die aus unterschiedlichen Kulturen stammenden Mitglieder der Schulen – SchülerInnen wie LehrerInnen – begrüßten die Idee der Inklusion an den Schulen ausdrücklich.

Die Daten der vier deutschen Schulen wurden in fünf separaten, einstündigen Interviews mit den SchulsozialarbeiterInnen erhoben, die jeweils an einer der drei Grundschulen und an der weiterführenden Schule geführt wurden. Die Interviews, bei denen jeweils zwei bis drei Mitglieder der Forschungsgruppe anwesend waren, wurden aufgezeichnet und transkribiert, um jedem Forschungsmitglied Einblick in die Daten zu ermöglichen und sie für den Forschungsbericht aufzubereiten.

4.5 Demografische Profile

4.5.1 Schule A (Grundschule)

Schule A ist eine inklusive Grundschule, die inklusive Praktiken fördert, damit die SchülerInnen ihre Talente und Bedürfnisse in ihrem eigenen Tempo entwickeln können. Die Schule strebt an, die Selbstlern- und Sozialkompetenz sowie laterales Denken zu unterstützen und regt zur Kreativität an. Sie ist davon überzeugt, dass ein Schulsystem, in dem Kinder ungeachtet ihrer Behinderung, Lernschwäche oder anderer Merkmale zusammen unterrichtet werden, wesentlich ist. Außerdem berücksichtigt die Schule die individuellen Bedürfnisse jedes Schülers und jeder Schülerin, ihre eigenen Ansichten und ihre Flexibilität bei der Gestaltung des Schulalltags um jedem Kind seinen eigenen Lernerfolg zu ermöglichen.

Schule A hat verfügt über neun LehrerInnen, einschließlich spezialisierter Lehrkräfte für Inklusion und Sonderpädagogik. Die Schule bietet eine flexible Anfangszeit für berufstätige Eltern an, sodass die SchülerInnen vor dem Unterricht spielen und die Zeit mit ihren FreundInnen verbringen können.

Die Schule hat keine festangestellten SchulsozialarbeiterInnen, verfügt aber über vier SonderpädagogInnen und vier LehrerInnen, die die individuellen Lehrpläne ausarbeiten und umsetzen. Das Kollegium sorgt dafür, dass die Schule als eine kleine Gemeinschaft reibungslos arbeitet. Da es keine feste Sozialarbeiterin oder einen festen Sozialarbeiter an der Schule gibt, ist sie stark auf die Kommunikation aller MitarbeiterInnen über die SchülerInnen angewiesen. Das Kollegium trifft sich jede Woche für eine Stunde zum Informationsaustausch, wobei die SonderpädagogInnen die anderen LehrerInnen mit Ratschlägen unterstützen, wie sie am besten auf die besonderen Bedürfnisse von SchülerInnen mit Behinderungen in ihrer Klasse eingehen können. Die Schule fördert die Beteiligung der Eltern am Schulleben, indem diese "für eine Stunde wöchentlich an der Schule arbeiten" (LehrerIn Schule A) und durch eine offene Anfangsphase von 7:30 – 8:30 die Möglichkeit haben sich regelmäßig mit den LehrerInnen auszutauschen. Eine Idee zur Inklusionsförderung ist zudem der "Morgenkreis" (LehrerIn Schule A), in dem die SchülerInnen zusammenkommen und mit einem "Redeball" darüber bestimmen, wer als nächster etwas sagen darf.

Die Schule verfügt über zahlreiche technische Einrichtungen mit dem Zweck, den Bedürfnissen aller SchülerInnen gerecht zu werden, wie etwa Treppen, Rampen und Aufzüge. Sie hat eine voll ausgestattete Küche mit eigenem

Koch, der das tägliche Mittagessen für die SchülerInnen zubereitet, sowie einen Speisesaal, in dem die Mahlzeiten gemeinsam in der Gruppe eingenommen oder auch nach eigenem Ermessen Snacks verzehrt werden können. Es gibt mehrere Zweckräume, in denen die SchülerInnen ihre Kreativität entfalten können, darunter einen Kunstraum, einen Raum für Holzarbeiten, einen Raum mit Bauklötzen und Spielzeug und einen Raum in welchem den SchülerInnen verschiedene Klettermöglichkeiten zur Verfügung stehen. Für die Räume sind keine bestimmten LehrerInnen abgestellt und die SchülerInnen sind bei ihren optionalen Aktivitäten dort weitestgehend unbeaufsichtigt. Von Zeit zu Zeit schaut eine Lehrkraft vorbei, um nachzusehen, ob die Kinder Unterstützung benötigen und ob es Ihnen gut geht.

Schule A war an externe BeobachterInnen im Unterricht gewöhnt, da sie als 'inklusive' Schule klassifiziert ist und regelmäßig zu Hospitationsterminen für Interessierte offen steht. Es wurde ein Zeitlimit von vier Stunden vereinbart, um die SchülerInnen so wenig wie möglich abzulenken, sodass alle Beobachtungen in diesem Zeitrahmen stattfinden mussten. Es war möglich, sämtliche Interaktionen der Kinder untereinander sowie ihre Erledigung der gestellten Aufgaben zu beobachten. Ebenfalls konnte beobachtet werden, in welchem Maße die Lehrkraft ihren Unterrichtsstil an die verschiedenen Kinder anpasste.

Die beobachtete Klasse der *Schule A* setzte sich aus SchülerInnen des ersten bis dritten Jahrgangs zusammen; der Unterricht fand in zwei Klassenräumen statt, in denen jeweils zwei Lehrpersonen für eine unterschiedliche Anzahl von Kindern zuständig waren. Es fiel auf, dass viele SchülerInnen während des Unterrichts auf dem Boden saßen und es keine typische 'Schultisch-Ordnung' gab. Im Klassenzimmer gab es nur einen Tisch mit sieben Stühlen, aber mehr als sieben Kinder, sodass nicht alle Kinder gleichzeitig darauf sitzen konnten. Es existierte zwar ein strukturierter Lehr und Stundenplan, die SchülerInnen konnten ihre Aufgaben jedoch jeweils frei wählen; manche Kinder streiften durch den Klassenraum und wandten sich wechselnden Aktivitäten oder Themen zu, die sie gerade interessierten. Die Rolle der LehrerInnen war dabei eher vermittelnd als erziehend: Sie redeten in ruhigem, sanftem Ton und ermunterten die Kinder zur Lösung der schwierigeren Probleme und offenen Fragen, die in ihren Aktivitäten und Projekten auftauchten. Die Idee des 'individualisierten Lernens', bei dem "die oder der Lernende in den Mittelpunkt des Lehrens, Lernens und Bewertens gestellt wird" (Jones & McLean 2012, S. 75) wird dadurch betont, dass die SchülerInnen keine standardisierten Berichte oder Noten erhalten, die ihren Fortschritt widerspiegeln, sondern vielmehr in regelmäßigen Gesprächen mit den Lehrenden darüber informiert werden, in welchen Bereichen sie erfolgreich sind und in welchen sie sich noch verbessern sollten. Um den Lernfortschritt der SchülerInnen zu überprüfen, betreut jede Lehrkraft acht SchülerInnen. Diese „Bezugsperson", beobachtet die Lernfortschritte dieser acht Kinder genau und bespricht mit Ihnen individuelle

Lehrpläne sowie tägliche Aufgabenübersichten, in denen aufgezeigt wird, was das einzelne Kind am jeweiligen Tag gemacht hat.

4.5.2 Schule B (Grundschule)

Schule B ist eine Grundschule, die es sich zur Aufhabe gemacht hat, alle Kinder des Stadtteils aufzunehmen. Unter 'inklusiver Pädagogik' versteht sie das Angebot "individueller Lernziele und differenzierter Aufgaben für alle SchülerInnen" (Schulsozialarbeiterin Schule B). Die Schule hat pro Klasse 23 SchülerInnen und insgesamt 23 Lehrkräfte, darunter eine Sonderpädagogin bzw. einen Sonderpädagogen und eine festangestellte Schulsozialarbeiterin. Die SchülerInnen können an selbstgewählten Workshops (Sport, Theater, Tanz) teilnehmen, um Eltern entgegenzukommen, die länger oder im Schichtdienst arbeiten.

In *Schule B* werden SchülerInnen des ersten bis vierten Jahrgangs gemeinsam in einer Klasse unterrichtet. Es gibt jeweils einen Klassenlehrer oder eine Klassenlehrerin und zusätzlich wechselnde UnterrichtsassistentInnen und HelferInnen. Die Schule stellt ehrenamtliche HelferInnen aus der näheren Umgebung als UnterrichtsassistentInnen ein, die allen SchülerInnen im Klassenraum Hilfestellungen bieten und darüber hinaus Tanz-, Theater-, Sport- und Musikangebote machen. Die Rolle der HelferInnen besteht darin, die SchülerInnen zu unterstützen und so die Klassenlehrerin/den Klassenlehrer zu entlasten. Dies wird dadurch erreicht, dass sie SchülerInnen mit Verhaltensauffälligkeiten, Lernbehinderungen oder -schwierigkeiten einzeln oder in Gruppen fördern.

Die Schule betont, dass jeder an ihr willkommen ist, was sich in der folgenden Aussage widerspiegelt: "Im Sinne einer inklusiven Schule heißen wir alle Menschen willkommen!" (Schulsozialarbeiterin Schule B). Die Schule ist in dem Sinne benachteiligt, dass ihr die Stadt keine "IntegrationshelferInnen" (Schulsozialarbeiterin Schule B) in den Klassen finanziert. Das Fehlen von Fördermitteln zeigt sich besonders dadurch, dass die LehrerInnen selbst für die Sauberkeit und Instandhaltung der Schule verantwortlich sind und dass die UnterrichtsassistentInnen und HelferInnen alle ehrenamtlich arbeiten.

Ein Merkmal der *Schule B* ist, dass alle SchülerInnen individuelle, auf sie zugeschnittene Aufgaben erledigen, obwohl sie in jahrgangsübergreifenden Klassen (1.-4. Jahrgang) unterrichtet werden. In den Fächern Mathematik und Englisch werden sie nach Leistungsfähigkeit eingeteilt, in allen anderen Fächern können sie selbst bestimmen, welche Aufgaben mit welchem Schwierigkeitsgrad sie wann bearbeiten wollen. Ein Team aus LehrerInnen, einer Sonderpädagogin/einem Sonderpädagogen und einer Sozialarbeiterin entwickelt die Lehrpläne für die SchülerInnen. Für jedes Kind werden individuelle soziale, verhaltensbezogene und akademische Förderpläne erstellt und umgesetzt. Die verhaltensbezogene und akademische Förderung findet durch Team-Teaching im Klassenraum statt und auch auf dem Schulhof arbeitet das Team zur Förderung des Sozialverhaltens zusammen, sodass die LehrerInnen den Fortschritt der SchülerInnen beobachten können. Das Team-Teaching trägt dazu bei, "eine dynamische und interaktive Lernumgebung zu schaffen" (Leavitt 2006, S.1) und kann die SchülerInnen dazu anregen, "beim Lernen von neuem Stoff ein höheres Maß an Synthese und Integration zu erreichen" (Leavitt 2006, S.2). Die Rolle der Lehrerin/des Lehrers ist die einer Vermittlerin/eines Vermittlers, die/der die SchülerInnen dabei unterstützt, ihre Arbeit fertigzustellen, individuelle Hilfe anbietet, wo es nötig ist, und sie motiviert, sich selbst zu fordern.

Es gehört zum Programm der Schule, dass ihre Traditionen, Regeln und Techniken von den älteren an die jüngeren Schülerinnen weitergegeben werden. Aus diesem Grund lernen die SchülerInnen in jahrgangsgemischten Gruppen. Das Mediatorenprogramm wurde unter andem von der Schulsozialarbeiterin umgesetzt. Mit diesem Programm lernen die SchülerInnen, im Klassenraum und auf dem Schulhof als Schlichter zu agieren. Es vermittelt ihnen "spezifische Kenntnisse und praktische Fähigkeiten von Mediatoren, Spiele und Übungen zur Stärkung des Selbstwertgefühls, das Vermögen, Gefühle zu erkennen und zu benennen, sowie Kooperationsfähigkeit" (Schulsozialarbeiterin Schule B). Die Kinder legen eine Prüfung ab, in der sie nachweisen müssen, dass sie sich ihrer Rolle bewusst sind. Sie sind auf dem Schulhof an gelben Warnwesten zu erkennen. Die Schule legt Wert darauf, dass "das gemeinsame Lernen voneinander an erster Stelle steht" (Schulsozialarbeiterin Schule B); das gibt den KlassenlehrerInnen und Hilfskräften die Möglichkeit, als 'Berater' zu agieren und verschafft ihnen mehr Zeit für die individuelle Arbeit mit dem Kind.

Die Rolle der Sozialarbeiterin
Schule B hat eine festangestellte Sozialarbeiterin, deren Rolle im Wesentlichen darin besteht, Eltern und SchülerInnen gleichermaßen in der Schulgemeinschaft zu unterstützen. In der Region, in der die Schule liegt, leben viele türkischstämmige Familien, die typischerweise einen geringen sozioökonomischen Status haben. Diese Familien sind darauf angewiesen, dass die Sozialarbeiterin ihnen Hilfen und Informationen über das Leben in Deutschland anbietet, darunter auch Möglichkeiten der finanziellen Unterstützung und Förderung.

4.5.3 Schule C (Grundschule)

Auch *Schule C* ist eine Grundschule; es gibt pro Klasse 25 SchülerInnen und insgesamt 36 LehrerInnen, einschließlich einer Sonderpädagogin und einer festangestellten Sozialarbeiterin

Schule B fördert Inklusion, indem sie alle SchülerInnen aufnimmt und ihnen dabei hilft, "Selbst-, Sozial- und Sachkompetenzen zu entwickeln, um in einer sich ständig verändernden Gesellschaft das eigene Leben gestalten und an der Weiterentwicklung des Gemeinwesens mitwirken zu können" (Leitbild Schule C). Des Weiteren fördert die Schule auch individualisiertes Lernen durch persönliche Wochenpläne, in denen die Lernaufgaben jeweils genau auf den Entwicklungsstand des Kindes zugeschnitten werden, und durch Gruppenarbeit.

Die Schule hat eine sonderpädagogische Förderklasse mit vier bis fünf SchülerInnen, die gemeinsam mit einer Klassenlehrerin/einem Klassenlehrer auf einer elementaren Ebene an Problemen in den Fächern Englisch und Mathematik sowie an alltagspraktischen Fähigkeiten arbeiten. Die Kinder in dieser Klasse müssen große Sprachbarrieren überwinden, da sie erst vor kurzer Zeit aus der Türkei, Griechenland oder Polen immigriert sind. Die Schule unterstützt sie auf vielfältige Weise, u.a. durch: die Einstellung von LehrerInnen, die ihre Muttersprache sprechen; die Erlaubnis, die Schule früher zu verlassen, wenn ein Kind keinen ganzen Schultag bewältigen kann; Hilfe bei Prüfungen: diese sind optional bzw. die Schule stellt geeignete Hilfen zur Verfügung, wie z.B. LeserInnen oder SchreiberInnen, um den Kindern eine faire Chance zu geben, die Prüfung erfolgreich absolvieren zu können.

Die SchülerInnen werden dazu je nach Fähigkeitsstufe zu verschiedenen Zeiten für jeweils eine Stunde am Tag aus ihren Klassen genommen und arbeiten in der Kleingruppe mit der Sonderpädagogin. In den Zeiten, in denen sie nicht in diesen Gruppen tätig ist, besucht die Sonderpädagogin die Klassen der anderen SchülerInnen mit besonderen Bedürfnissen. Für zwei Stunden in der Woche unterstützt sie so die jeweilige Klassenlehrerin/den Klassenlehrer. Die Schule legt großen Wert auf Zusammenarbeit und die Sonderpädagogin führt gemeinsam mit der Sozialarbeiterin und dem Klassenlehrer/der Klassenlehrerin Entwicklungsgespräche und erstellt individuelle Lernpläne für alle SchülerInnen. Gemeinsam werden für jedes Kind drei Ziele festgesetzt, die es in den nächsten sechs bis acht Wochen erreichen soll. Die Leistungen werden anhand eines Punktesystems belohnt, was auch zu einer Befreiung von den Hausarbeiten führen kann. Die KlassenlehrerInnen helfen den SchülerInnen durch beständiges Loben und Ermutigen, ihre Ziele zu erreichen. Sie achten darauf, dass die Ziele, die die Kinder sich selbst setzen, auch erreichbar sind. Nach jeder Stunde werden die Wochenpunkte der SchülerInnen aktualisiert, um Verbesserungen aufzuzeigen und zu bestimmen, ob sich ein Kind einen hausaufgabenfreien Tag verdient hat.

Die *Schule B* tut viel dafür, den familiären Hintergrund ihrer SchülerInnen in deren Lernumgebung mit einzubeziehen. Ein wirksames Hilfsmittel dazu ist eine Weltkarte an einer der Schulwände, auf der der ursprüngliche Herkunftsort und der kulturelle Hintergrund der Kinder markiert ist. Die Sozialarbeiterin bezieht die Familien der SchülerInnen in ihre Arbeit mit ein, um ihnen so ein Gefühl der Zugehörigkeit zu vermitteln und gewisse Organisationsstrukturen vorzugeben. Da es im Leben der Familien immer wieder zu schwierigen und alleine nicht zu bewältigenden Problemen kommen kann, macht die Sozialarbeiterin regelmäßig Hausbesuche und bietet professionelle Hilfe bei bestimmten Problemen an, wie etwa der Arbeitssuche oder der Beantragung finanzieller Unterstützung und anderer Hilfen.

Die Rolle der Sozialarbeiterin
Die Sozialarbeiterin ist auf die persönliche Beziehung zu Eltern und SchülerInnen angewiesen, da sich nur so das nötige Vertrauensverhältnis entwickeln kann.. Die Sozialarbeiterin kann auch Gruppen von fünf bis sechs SchülerInnen auf eine 'Traumreise' mitnehmen, das heißt, die Kinder können sich für etwa 45 Minuten auf einem Wasserbett bei gedämpftem Licht und beruhigender Musik entspannen.

Die Sozialarbeiterin ist stark in das tägliche Geschehen der Klasse eingebunden und bespricht Fragen mit den KlassenlehrerInnen, um individuelle Handlungspläne für die SchülerInnen zu entwickeln. SchulsozialarbeiterInnen und KlassenlehrerInnen "sind bei der Dokumentation von Problemen, Leistungen und Herausforderungen sehr auf einander angewiesen" (Schulsozialarbeiterin Schule C). Daneben hat die Schulsozialarbeiterin auch noch andere Aufgaben an der Schule; sie bietet eigene Unterrichtseinheiten an, in denen die Kinder lernen können, besser mit Stress und Drucksituationen umzugehen und ihre Sozialkompetenz zu verbessern. Dieser Unterricht findet während der normalen Schulzeit statt. Die SchülerInnen werden dazu aus ihren normalen Klassen genommen und entweder im Büro der Sozialarbeiterin oder in einem extra für diesen Zweck freigehaltenen Klassenraum unterrichtet.

Die Schulsozialarbeiterin arbeitet mit dem Jugendamt zusammen und vermittelt bei Konflikten oder Problemen zwischen den SchülerInnen. In den Pausen hält sie sich auf dem Schulhof auf, regt Spiele an und fördert positive soziale Interaktionen unter den SchülerInnen. Diesen bietet sich so die Gelegenheit, in der unterrichtsfreien Zeit mit der Sozialarbeiterin ins Gespräch zu kommen. LehrerInnen und SchulsozialarbeiterInnen an der Schule sind zur Vertraulichkeit und zum Schutz der Privatsphäre ihrer SchülerInnen verpflichtet. Es kann sein, dass die Klassenlehrerin die genauen Familienverhältnisse oder die persönlichen Probleme eines Kindes nicht kennt, und ebenso muss die Schulsozialarbeiterin nicht notwendigerweise über die Lernschwierigkeiten eines Kindes informiert sein (Schulsozialarbeiterin Schule C).

4.5.4 Vergleich

An allen drei Schulen arbeitet die Schulsozialarbeiterin jeweils sowohl in Gruppen als auch individuell mit den SchülerInnen; die Arbeit findet entweder im Klassenraum statt, oder die Kinder werden für Sozialtraining-Stunden aus der Klasse herausgenommen. Während des Sozialkompetenztrainings sollen die SchülerInnen ihre sozialen Kompetenzen stärken, das heißt, die Kommunikation und Interaktion mit anderen verbessern. Eine weitere Aufgabe der Sozialarbeiterin war es, den SchülerInnen dabei zu helfen, Freundschaften mit ihresgleichen aufzubauen und aufrechtzuerhalten, indem sie sie gemäß ihren Interessen miteinander in Kontakt brachte. Sie brachte die SchülerInnen paarweise oder, wenn sie selbstsicherer im Umgang mit ihren Altersgenossen waren, in Gruppen zusammen. Die Sozialkompetenz wurde dann mit lockeren Brainstorming-Runden weiter gefördert, in denen die SchülerInnen den Mut und das Selbstvertrauen erlernen konnten, um dann auf dem Schulhof oder in der Klasse selbst leichter Freundschaften schließen zu können.

Snoezel-Räume

An zwei der drei Grundschulen gibt Entspannungs- bzw. Snoezel-Räume. Dabei handelt es sich um Orte in der Schule, an denen die SchülerInnen sich während ihrer Pausen einzeln oder in kleinen Gruppen von bis zu sechs Kindern auf Betten oder Sitzsäcke legen und schlafen oder ruhen können. Darüber hinaus können die SchulsozialarbeiterInnen auch SchülerInnen aus ihren Klassen holen und mit ihnen im Snoezel-Raum arbeiten; dort lernen sie zum Beispiel zu meditieren oder belastende Erfahrungen zu bewältigen. Die SchülerInnen haben auch die Möglichkeit dort zu schlafen, die besonders dann genutzt wird, wenn die Eltern nachts arbeiten und die Kinder auf ihre kleineren Geschwister aufpassen müssen. In jeder der Schulen war die Sozialarbeiterin für diese Räume verantwortlich und der Aufenthalt in diesen Räumen wurde allerseits als Privileg für die SchülerInnen betrachtet.

An der *Schule B* war der Snoezel-Raum in den Pausen frei zugänglich und bis zu sechs Kinder konnten sich darin aufhalten. Eine Beaufsichtigung durch das Lehrpersonal war nicht erforderlich, weil sich das LehrerInnenzimmer direkt gegenüber und damit in Hörweite befand. Der Raum wurde als stiller Ruheraum betrachtet, in dem die SchülerInnen der hektischen Schulhofatmosphäre entfliehen und sich in den Schulpausen und während der Mittagszeit entspannen konnten. An der *Schule C* mussten die Kinder in Gruppen von der Schulsozialarbeiterin in den Raum geführt werden, weil dieser von den anderen Klassenräumen abgelegen lag und ohne Schlüssel nicht zugänglich war. Hier wurde er als Arbeitsraum betrachtet, in dem die Sozialarbeiterin sich mit den SchülerInnen beschäftigen und ihnen ein Gefühl der Sicherheit vermitteln konnte. Die Kinder wurden dazu aus ihren Klassen genommen, konnten sich bei gedämpftem Licht auf ein Wasserbett legen und die Sozialarbeiterin leitete Meditationsübungen an, um ihnen zu helfen, sich zu entspannen und belastende oder beängstigende Situationen zu verarbeiten.

4.5.5 Weiterführende Schule D

Schule D hat pro Klasse 25 SchülerInnen und verfügt über zwei festangestellte SchulsozialarbeiterInnen. Die Schule nimmt Kinder ab dem zehnten Lebensjahr auf; nach dem zwölften Schuljahr können sie mit dem Abitur die allgemeine Hochschulreife erwerben.

Wegen des begrenzten Zeitraums der Datenerhebung war die *Schule D* die einzige weiterführende Schule, die untersucht werden konnte. Mit der Aufnahme dieser Schulform in die Untersuchung sollte eine Möglichkeit geschaffen werden, die Umsetzung des Inklusionskonzepts mit der an den Grundschulen zu vergleichen. Die Schule bot die Möglichkeit zu beobachten, wie die SchülerInnen den Übergang von der Grundschule bewältigten und wie sie sich in das neue Schulsystem einfügten.

Nicht alle weiterführenden Schulen in Deutschland beschäftigen SchulsozialarbeiterInnen, an der *Schule D* gab es jedoch aufgrund der hohen Schülerzahl von 1.000 Kindern deren zwei.

Die *Schule D* unterstützt die Idee der Inklusion, und obwohl "behinderte und nichtbehinderte Kinder zusammen unterrichtet werden", gibt es nur "eine Inklusionsklasse" (SchulsozialarbeiterIn Schule D). Die Inklusionsklasse umfasst ungefähr zwölf Unterrichtsstunden pro Woche und wird von einer Sonderpädagogin bzw. einem Sonderpädagogen betreut.

Die Rolle der SozialarbeiterInnen
Die Schule beschäftigt einen Sozialarbeiter und eine Sozialarbeiterin. Zu ihren Aufgaben gehört die Planung und Durchführung sozialer Programme für SchülerInnen, die Probleme im Umgang mit ihren AltersgenossInnen haben; daneben vermitteln sie Lebenskompetenzen in den Bereichen Drogenprävention, Umgang mit Sexualität oder klären über die Wirkung von Alkohol auf.

Die SchulsozialarbeiterInnen sind nicht gleichrangig (der Sozialarbeiter ist der Vorgesetzte), aber beide bieten individuelle Beratung für LehrerInnen, SchülerInnen und Eltern an, unterstützen die KlassenlehrerInnen und begleiten die Kinder bei Ausflügen.

Der Sozialarbeiter plant und leitet Informationsveranstaltungen und Arbeitsgruppen für Eltern zu aktuellen Themen wie Alkoholkonsum, 'Sexting' (das Versenden von Nacktfotos per SMS oder Internet) oder dem Umgang mit Drucksituationen wie Abschlussprüfungen, wobei er auch die Maßgaben und Erwartungen der Schule deutlich macht. Er ist auch für die Durchführung von Ferienaktivitäten zuständig, mit denen das Interesse der SchülerInnen an der Schule auch in der Ferienzeit aufrechterhalten und ihre Sozialkompetenz gesteigert werden soll; die Sozialarbeiterin assistiert ihm dabei und ist ebenfalls bei den Ferienaktivitäten präsent um die SchülerInnen zusätzlich zu unterstützen. Beide bieten nach der Schule ein Nachmittagsprogramm für alle SchülerInnen an, in denen sie ihre Schulaufgeben machen und bei Bedarf besondere Förderung erhalten können; außerdem werden die Kinder ermuntert, in den Schulsportmannschaften aktiv zu werden und sich an den sonstigen Aktivitäten der Schule zu beteiligen.

Die SchulsozialarbeiterInnen arbeiten eng mit den KlassenlehrerInnen zusammen und besprechen sich täglich, um zum Wohl und im Interesse des Kindes agieren zu können. In der angesprochenen „Inklusionsklasse" sind fünf Kinder mit sonderpädagogischem Förderbedarf. Die LehrerInnen dieser Klasse haben eine Zusatzausbildung in inklusiven Praktiken, was eine schulweit einheitliche Praxis gewährleistet. Die Schule beschäftigt keine UnterrichtsassistentInnen, weil das Integrationsteam auf dem Standpunkt steht, dass sich das mit der Unterstützung hilfebedürftiger SchülerInnen innerhalb der Klasse verknüpfte Stigma negativ auf das Selbstwertgefühl und das Selbstvertrauen der SchülerInnen auswirkt (SchulsozialarbeiterIn Schule D).

Der Sozialarbeiter lädt Eltern mit Migrationshintergrund persönlich zum Besuch der Klasse ein, um ihnen innerhalb der schulischen Umgebung ein Gefühl der 'sozialen Inklusion' zu vermitteln, und kümmert sich um Gelder für SchülerInnen, die als ÜbersetzerInnen für Eltern fungieren, die Schwierigkeiten mit der deutschen oder englischen Sprache haben. Eine der größten Barrieren zwischen dem Sozialarbeiter und den SchülerInnen ist das Gefühl der 'Peinlichkeit' (Schulsozialarbeiter Schule D), das manchmal entsteht, etwa wenn es einer Schülerin unangenehm ist, persönliche Informationen gegenüber einem Mann zu äußern, und sie daher warten muss, bis die Sozialarbeiterin Zeit für sie hat. Bei SchülerInnen, die besonders gute schulische Leistungen erbringen, kann der Sozialarbeiter dafür sorgen, dass sie während der Schulzeit Lehrveranstaltungen an der Universität besuchen können. Dieses Angebot betrifft die letzten Schuljahre; wenn etwa eine Schülerin oder ein Schüler herausragende Fähigkeiten in Informatik zeigt und diesen Weg weitergehen möchte, ist es ihr oder ihm dank einer Kooperation mit der Universität möglich, sich bereits vor dem Schulabschluss für bestimmte Kurse einzuschreiben.

4.5.6 Auswertung der Daten

Die visuelle Ethnographie ist mit visuellen Bildern und Metaphern verknüpft und wurde in dieser Studie als eine Beobachtungsform benutzt. Die "visuelle Ethnographie" (Pink 2007, S. 22) als Methode ist ein Konzept, das Fotografien oder Bilder benutzt, um Beobachtungen zu unterstützen. Berg (2008, S. 935) erläutert, dass die verschiedenen Formen der visuellen Darstellung "ein Mittel zur Aufzeichnung, Dokumentation und Erklärung der sozialen Welten und Auffassungen von Menschen" bieten; außerdem fügen sie dem allgemein gebräuchlichen "verbalen Medium" ein "visuelles Medium" hinzu. Keegan (2008, S. 620) legt dar, dass visuelle Darstellungen "das gesprochene Wort ergänzen und häufig ein ergiebigeres, ganzheitlicheres Verständnis der Welten der Studienteilnehmer ermöglichen".

Der Einsatz der visuellen Ethnographie ermöglichte es der Forscherin, die Rollen und die Art und Weise, wie die SchulsozialarbeiterInnen ihre Zeit mit den Lernenden in der Klasse verbrachten, zu untersuchen. Die Forscherin konnte die SchulsozialarbeiterInnen bei der Benutzung von Therapieräumen beobachten und die Gestaltung der Klassen-, Musik- und Kunsträume in der Schule in Augenschein nehmen, die sich förderlich auf das Lernen der SchülerInnen innerhalb des Grundschulsystems auswirken sollen.

In Übereinstimmung mit der Idee der visuellen Ethnographie machte die Forscherin eine Reihe von Digitalfotografien der Schulen, die eine Kontextualisierung der Interviews und der Beobachtungsdaten aus einer visuellen Perspektive ermöglichten. Da das Hauptaugenmerk der Untersuchung auf inklusiven Praktiken in der Klasse lag, war es wichtig, die Gestaltung und den Aufbau der Klassenräume in Bezug zur Lernumgebung aus der Sicht der LehrerInnen und SchulsozialarbeiterInnen zu berücksichtigen.

4.5.7 Zusammenfassung

Die Beobachtungen, Notizen, Fotografien, Interviews und Diskussionen waren hilfreich, um einen Einblick in das deutsche Bildungssystem zu bekommen und zu verstehen, welche Rolle SchulsozialarbeiterInnen im Leben der SchülerInnen spielen. Um die wichtige Rolle der SchulsozialarbeiterInnen an deutschen Schulen vollständig zu erfassen, ist es erforderlich, das deutsche Bildungssystem zu verstehen. Ebenso wichtig ist das Verständnis des australischen Bildungssystems, insbesondere in New South Wales, um die beiden Systeme richtig vergleichen und analysieren zu können.

4.6 Diskussion

4.6.1 Das deutsche Bildungssystem:

Im traditionellen deutschen Schulsystem werden die SchülerInnen nach der Grundschule gemäß ihrer akademischen Fähigkeiten und späteren Berufsabsichten getrennt. Nach der vierten Klasse, mit zehn Jahren, müssen sie sich entscheiden, welche weiterführende Schule sie besuchen wollen. Das Gymnasium ist für SchülerInnen gedacht, die sich auf eine tertiäre Ausbildung an einer Universität vorbereiten wollen. Diese traditionelle Struktur schafft Uneinigkeit, denn die Schule nimmt vorwiegend die Kinder mit den besten Noten auf. Damit wirkt diese Praxis der Idee der Inklusion grundsätzlich entgegen. Seit 2013 haben einige Gymnasien, wie etwa auch die *Schule D*, damit begonnen, SchülerInnen mit Behinderungen und Lernschwierigkeiten aufzunehmen, und haben ihre Lern- und Unterrichtsinhalte an die individuellen Bedürfnisse dieser SchülerInnen angepasst.

Die *Schule D* unterstützt das Konzept der Inklusion und der dortige Sozialarbeiter stellte stolz fest, dass "die Anmeldungen von SchülerInnen mit Behinderungen oder Lernschwierigkeiten für das neue Schuljahr 2014 gestiegen sind" (Schulsozialarbeiter Schule D). Er erklärte auch, dass nicht alle LehrerInnen der Schule hinter der Umsetzung der Inklusionsidee stünden, da viele so sehr an das hohe Leistungsniveau der SchülerInnen gewöhnt seien, dass sie sich nicht ausreichend vorbereitet fühlten, um die Aufgaben an Kinder mit einem niedrigeren Leistungsniveau oder mit Hör- oder Sehbehinderungen anzupassen und zu differenzieren. Auf ihrer wöchentlich stattfindenden Konferenz äußerten die LehrerInnen auch, dass sie sich häufig "verurteilt" fühlten, wenn Unterstützungskräfte in ihre Klassen kommen müssten, um einzelnen SchülerInnen zu helfen. Des Weiteren beschäftigte die *Schule D* die Frage, wie sie es schaffen soll, ihre knappen Finanzmittel so umzuverteilen, dass sie auch SchülerInnen mit besonderen Bedürfnissen gerecht werden kann. Der Sozialarbeiter erklärte beispielsweise, dass die Schule für alle SchülerInnen einer Klasse Headsets mit Mikrofonen anschaffen musste, um ein Kind mit einer Hörbehinderung in die Lage zu versetzen, dem Unterricht zu folgen und LehrerInnen wie SchülerInnen zu verstehen.

Die vier besuchten Schulen arbeiteten unter anderem nach dem Prinzip der Montessoripädagogik (Montessori, 2014), der "Unabhängigkeit fördert, indem er eine Umgebung aus Aktivitäten und Materialien bereitstellt, welche Kinder in ihrer eigenen Geschwindigkeit nutzen können" (Montessori Australia, o.J.). Das deutsche Bildungssystem hat viele Vorzüge, dazu zählen unter anderem das differenzierte Curriculum und die effektive Nutzung des projektbasierten Lernens. Dieses versetzt die SchülerInnen in die Lage, den Prozess des Nachforschens zu durchlaufen, um die Antwort auf eine Frage, ein Problem oder eine Herausforderung zu finden. Alle LehrerInnen der vier untersuchten deutschen Schulen planten, leiteten und bewerteten die Fortschritte ihrer SchülerInnen. Des Weiteren förderten sie die Zusammenarbeit und Kommunikation der Kinder sowohl untereinander als auch mit dem Lehrpersonal.

Eine weitere Stärke des deutschen Bildungssystems ist, dass die SchulzozialarbeiterInnen eine aktive Rolle im Leben der Kinder spielen. Sie sind für die folgenden Aufgaben an der Schule zuständig:
i) Organisation von Aktivitäten für die SchülerInnen in den Ferien und nach Schulschluss;
ii) gemeinsames Team-Teaching mit den LehrerInnen;
iii) Unterstützung der SchülerInnen beim Aufbau von Freundeskreisen innerhalb und außerhalb der Klasse;
iv) Förderung des Selbstwertgefühls und der Sozialkompetenz der SchülerInnen;
v) Überprüfung der korrekten Weitergabe von Informationen der Schule an die Eltern;
vi) Hausbesuche bei SchülerInnen, um deren Lebensbedingungen und häusliches Umfeld einschätzen zu können;
vii) Diskussionen mit Eltern über die Bildungschancen ihrer Kinder; und
viii) Beratung der Eltern über finanzielle bzw. persönliche Unterstützungsmöglichkeiten (Schulsozialarbeiter Schule D).

Alle befragten SchulsozialarbeiterInnen gaben an, dass sie "während der Pausen und in der Mittagszeit draußen sind" (SchulsozialarbeiterInnen B, C, D), um sich den SchülerInnen bekannt zu machen und sie zum gemeinsamen Spielen zu ermutigen. Alle waren nach eigenen Angaben auch immer für die Kinder erreichbar. Schulsozialarbeiterin C (2013)und Schulsozialarbeiterin B (2013) erklärte: "Ich sitze oft in meinem Büro. Viele sagen, die Schulsozialarbeiterin sitzt nur in ihrem Büro. Es klopfen aber jeden Tag Kinder an, um einfach nur zu reden." Der/die SchulsozialarbeiterIn D und der/die LehrerIn der Schule A wurden während eines Schulbesuchstages beobachtet, wie sie während der Pausen und in der Mittagszeit mit verschiedenen SchülerInnengruppen diskutierten.

Finanzielle Not und Scheidung spielten bei den SchülerInnen der besuchten Schulen eine große Rolle, da diese allesamt in sozialökonomisch benachteiligten Gegenden lagen und viele der Eltern lange arbeiten mussten und wenig Zeit für die Beaufsichtigung ihrer Kinder hatten. Die Kinder brachten viele ihrer persönlichen Probleme mit in die Schule und diese wurden von den SchulsozialarbeiterInnen permanent angesprochen. So erklärte die Schulsozialarbeiterin B (2013): "Wir sind hier in einer benachteiligten Gegend und die Kinder bringen viele massive Probleme mit in die Schule." Einige Schülerinnen der Schule B bekannten, dass "meine Mutter Alkoholikerin ist und ich sexuell missbraucht wurde". Die Aussage stammt aus einem Gespräch der Sozialarbeiterin mit zwei achtjährigen

Mädchen. year old girls. Darüber hinaus leiten die SchulsozialarbeiterInnen die "nachschulische Betreuung" (Schulsozialarbeiterin Schule C) und die "Organisation von Arbeitsgruppen im Nachmittagsbereich" (Schulsozialarbeiter Schule D). Das deutsche Bildungssystem ermuntert alle Eltern, sich an der Bildung ihrer Kinder zu beteiligen und eine wichtige Rolle in der Schulgemeinschaft zu spielen. Nach Aussage einer Lehrerin der Schule A (2013) "haben die Eltern der SchülerInnen an dieser Schule einen vierzehntägigen Plan mit allen Aufgaben und Diensten, die im Rahmen der Schule zu erledigen sind". Typischerweise umfassten solche Elterndienste das freiwillige Reinigen der Klassenräume, die Unterstützung von SchülerInnen bei Grundlagen des Lesens und Rechnens (vergleichbar mit der Rolle einer Unterrichtsassistentin oder eines Unterrichtsassistenten), den Besuch von Schulversammlungen mit ihren Kindern und die Hilfen beim Aufbau von Geräten oder der Ausstattung von Räumlichkeiten für die SchülerInnen. An der Schule A oblag beispielsweise die Ausstattung der Fachklassenräume für Musik und Kunst sowie die Reinigung der normalen Klassenräume samt Tischen, Stühlen und Außenspielbereich ausschließlich den LehrerInnen und Eltern. An Schule B erklärte die dortige Schulsozialarbeiterin (2013), dass "die Instandhaltung und Reinigung im Bereich der Schule vollständig von den LehrerInnen erledigt wird", die gleichzeitig ihren Unterricht vorbereiten und abhalten müssen.

Die besuchten deutschen Schulen versuchen durch jahrgangsübergreifende Klassen SchülerInnen verschiedener Altersstufen und Schuljahre in das Lernen der Kinder zu integrieren. An der Grundschule B "bestehen die Klassen aus Kindern des ersten bis vierten Jahrgangs" und es gibt höchstens "23 Kinder pro Klasse" (Schulsozialarbeiterin Schule B). Ähnlich werden an der Grundschule A "die Jahrgänge eins bis drei kombiniert" (LehrerIn Schule A) und an Schule C ist es ebenso (Schulsozialarbeiterin C). Diese Vermischung der verschiedenen Jahrgängr wurde als hilfreich für Geschwisterkinder angesehen, da die älteren den jüngeren die korrekten Abläufe an der Schule beibringen konnten, wie etwa das Aufstellen vor der Klasse, das Betreten des Klassenraums, das Auspacken ihrer Sachen oder das Schuheausziehen vor der Begrüßung der Klassenlehrerin oder des Klassenlehrers.

4.6.2 Das Bildungssystem in NSW:

Die Schulen in New South Wales beschäftigen keine SchulsozialarbeiterInnen, sondern BeratungslehrerInnen. Diese spielen eine zentrale Rolle für die Entwicklung und die Befindlichkeit vieler SchülerInnen, insbesondere derer mit Lernbehinderungen oder -schwierigkeiten. Wie weiter oben ausgeführt, definiert das NSW DEC die Rolle und den Aufgabenbereich der BeratungslehrerInnen an Schulen wie folgt:

- Beratung von SchülerInnen;
- Förderung des Lernens und des Wohlbefindens der SchülerInnen in Absprache mit den anderen MitarbeiterInnen der Schule;
- Abgabe kognitiver, sozialer und verhaltensbezogener Beurteilungen der SchülerInnen;
- Beteiligung an der Entwicklung und Planung für SchülerInnen mit besonderen Bedürfnissen;
- Vermittlung von SchülerInnen und deren Familien an andere zur Förderung der Gesundheit und des Wohlbefindens der SchülerInnen und ihrer Familien notwendige Stellen und Unterstützungseinrichtungen (NSW DEC, o.J., S. 3).

Es erscheint evident, dass die BeratungslehrerInnen in NSW eine weniger aktive, praktische und auffällige Rolle spielen als die SchulsozialarbeiterInnen in Deutschland. Zu den Aufgaben, die beiden gemeinsam sind, gehören Beratung, Intervention, Vermittlung sozialer Kompetenzen und die schulische Unterstützung der Kinder. Ebenfalls bieten beide Informationen und zusätzliche Hilfen für SchülerInnen und deren Eltern, wenn ihnen der Zugang zu Ressourcen oder spezielle Fähigkeiten zur Unterstützung des Kindes fehlen. Ein Punkt, in dem sich die beiden Rollen deutlich unterscheiden, ist die Einbeziehung des heimischen Umfeldes der Kinder: Den BeratungslehrerInnen in NSW ist jeder Kontakt zu den SchülerInnen außerhalb der Schulzeit untersagt; anders als die SchulsozialarbeiterInnen in Deutschland dürfen sie die SchülerInnen nicht zuhause besuchen oder deren private Situation bewerten.

Daneben gibt es noch eine Reihe weiterer Unterschiede zwischen den Rollen und Aufgaben der SchulsozialarbeiterInnen in Deutschland und der BeratungslehrerInnen in NSW.

Die BeratungslehrerInnen müssen die Kinder in den Pausen nicht auf dem Schulhof beaufsichtigen. Die BeratungslehrerInnen in NSW arbeiten auch nicht im Klassenraum; es ist dort die Aufgabe von BetreuungslehrerInnen, die gemeinsam mit den KlassenlehrerInnen in der Klasse unterrichten, für wichtig erachtete Informationen an die BeratungslehrerInnen weiterzugeben. Alle Probleme von KlassenlehrerInnen mit SchülerInnen werden an die BeratungslehrerInnen weitergeleitet. In Deutschland haben die SchülerInnen entsprechend die Möglichkeit, mit den SchulsozialarbeiterInnen zu reden, wenn sie mit inner- oder außerschulischen Situationen Probleme haben.

Ein wichtiges Merkmal des australischen Bildungssystems ist, dass Eltern von Kindern mit Behinderungen oder Lernschwierigkeiten zum größten Teil selbst verantwortlich sind und die Initiative ergreifen müssen, um dem Kind den

Zugang zu den Ressourcen und Hilfen zu ermöglichen, die sie für eine vollständige Inklusion in die Regelklasse benötigen. Diese Eltern sind damit einem großen Druck ausgesetzt, da viele gar nicht wissen, welche externen Angebote für ihr Kind in Frage kommen und für seine Schullaufbahn förderlich wären.

Der 2014 erschienene neue Lehrplan *National Curriculum for Australia* für die Fächer Englisch, Mathematik, Naturwissenschaften und Geschichte der Jahrgangsstufen fünf und sechs wird von vielen Pädagogen als ein Schwachpunkt im Bildungssystem von NSW gesehen; ein landesweites Curriculum bedeutet zwar, dass allen SchülerInnen in Australien die gleichen Inhalte vermittelt werden, es lässt aber auch keinerlei Differenzierungen zu. Das *National Curriculum* ist für die meisten Bereiche verbindlich, was LehrerInnen nicht gerade dazu ermutigt, innovativ zu sein und projektbasierten Unterricht zu Themen, die ihre SchülerInnen mehr interessieren würden, anzubieten. Das australische Curriculum informiert die LehrerInnen auch nicht darüber, wie alternative und moderne Unterrichtsmethoden in die Praxis umgesetzt werden können und sollen. Das australische Bildungssystem sollte sich an das deutsche anpassen, in dem projektbasiertes Lernen und die Differenzierung des Lehrplans gängige Praxis sind. Der Ansatz des projektbasierten Lernens macht Ressourcen zugänglich, die auf die speziellen Bedürfnisse der SchülerInnen ausgerichtet sind, die von ihren LehrerInnen angeleitet werden, am Forschungsprozess mitzuwirken, um ein Ergebnis zu erzielen.

4.6.3 Empfehlungen für die Zukunft

Aus dem Vergleich mit dem deutschen Bildungssystem lässt sich eine Reihe von Empfehlungen ableiten, die das Bildungsministerium in NSW für seine Schulpolitik und die tägliche Praxis an Grund- und weiterführenden Schulen in Erwägung ziehen sollte. Zum einen sollte man die Rolle und die Beteiligung von Eltern und LehrerInnen in der Schulgemeinschaft überdenken, um zu einem die ganze Schule umfassenden, gemeinschaftlichen Lernen im Sinne der Schülerinnen und Schüler zu gelangen. Das deutsche Bildungssystem vertritt eine auf die Lernenden ausgerichtete und von ihnen ausgehende Pädagogik, für die etwa die Montessori-Idee steht. Indem man den SchülerInnen den Freiraum gibt, nach ihren eigenen Bedingungen zu lernen, wird es möglich, dass die LehrerInnen ein größeres Maß an Lern- und Lehrmethoden in ihren Lehrplan aufnehmen, wie etwa die Theorie der multiplen Intelligenzen oder die Lernzieltaxonomie nach Bloom (1972). Das Curriculum würde dadurch für SchülerInnen attraktiver und interessanter, was wiederum zu einer stärkeren Beteiligung und größeren Lernerfolgen führen könnte. Durch verschiedene Unterrichtsstile können die SchülerInnen auch ihr Lernen variieren und den Stil auswählen, der ihren Bedürfnissen am besten entspricht und mit dem sie in ihrem eigenen Tempo arbeiten können. SchülerInnen, die eher projektbasiert und eigenständig lernen, können ihre Bildungsbedürfnisse eher ausdrücken und sich Gehör verschaffen, was in traditionellen und konventionellen Schulformen häufig vermisst wird. Dies ist ein wichtiger Punkt, da das derzeit in der Entwicklung befindliche neue australische Curriculum den Schwerpunkt normativ auf die Leistung der SchülerInnen legt, was von vielen PädagogInnen kritisiert wird, weil es die Vielfalt und Differenzierung des Lernens einschränkt.

Es wurde beobachtet, dass sich die Differenzierung von Unterrichtsstilen und -präferenzen bei den Lerninhalten in den besuchten Schulen positiv auswirkt. Die SchülerInnen mussten nicht ermuntert werden, ihre Aufgaben fertigzustellen, weil sie ihre Themen und Lernfelder, über die sie etwas erfahren und die sie weiterverfolgen wollten, selbst gewählt hatten.

Ein weiteres Merkmal des deutschen Bildungssystems, das sich in NSW übernehmen ließe, ist die Idee des Lernens durch Handeln (*Learning by Doing*) und der Versuch seitens der Lehrenden, den SchülerInnen Spaß und Freude am Lernen zu vermitteln. Es wurde beobachtet, dass die deutschen LehrerInnen die Lerninhalte in spielerische Forschungsaufgaben verpackten; statt den SchülerInnen also explizit mitzuteilen, was sie lernten, wurden sie dazu ermutigt, investigative Problemlösungsstrategien anzuwenden. Dadurch wurden die SchülerInnen stärker in den eigenen Lernprozess eingebunden und in den Klassen gab es weniger Probleme mit Verhaltensauffälligkeiten. In Anbetracht des Erfolgs dieser Unterrichtsstrategie sollten die zuständigen Stellen in NSW darüber nachdenken, ähnliche Strategien in allen Klassen der australischen Primary und Secondary Schools einzuführen, um die Eigenbeteiligung der SchülerInnen zu fördern und weniger Verhaltensauffälligkeiten in den Klassen zu erleben.

Das deutsche Bildungssystem muss seine Bemühungen zur Förderung und Ausweitung der Inklusion fortsetzen und weiterhin LehrerInnen wie Schulen über den Nutzen der Inklusion für alle aufklären. Ein Problem, welches das Forschungsteam an den deutschen Bildungseinrichtungen feststellte, war die Aufteilung der SchülerInnen in die weiterführenden Schulen im Alter von zehn Jahren. Kinder mit Behinderungen und/oder Lernschwierigkeiten wurden früher nicht zum Gymnasium zugelassen und konnten diese Schulform daher aufgrund ihrer Beeinträchtigungen nicht wählen. Seit 2013 nehmen einige Gymnasien alle SchülerInnen ungeachtet ihrer schulischen Leistungsfähigkeit auf. Diese Entwicklung sollte weiter verfolgt werden um ein inklusives Schulsystem weiter auszubauen. Dazu müsste das deutsche Bildungssystem nicht nur dafür sorgen, dass alle Kinder die Chance erhalten, die Schule ihrer Wahl zu besuchen, sondern auch dafür, dass die Inklusion innerhalb der Schulen gefördert wird und diese genügend Fördermittel erhalten, um allen Bedürfnissen der SchülerInnen und ihrer LehrerInnen gerecht werden zu können.

4.7 Literatur

Ashman, A. F., Elkins J. (2012). Education for inclusion and diversity. Frenchs Forest, NSW Pearson
A
Australian Government Department of Health Services (2013) *Social Work Services*. Retrieved from http://www.humanservices.gov.au/customer/services/centrelink/social-work-services
Australian Institute of Health and Welfare (2013) *Definition of Disability*. Retrieved from https://www.aihw.gov.au/definition-of-disability/
Bloom, B.(Hrsg.) (1972). Taxonomie von Lernzielen im kognitiven Bereich. 4. Auflage. Beltz Verlag, Weinheim und Basel
Berg, B (2008) The SAGE Encyclopedia of Qualitative Research Methods. Given, L. http://dx.doi.org.ezproxy.une.edu.au/10.4135/9781412963909
Cologon, K (2003). *Inclusion in Education: towards equality for students with disability*. Sydney, Australia: Children and Families Research Centre, Institute of Early Childhood Macquarie University
Dixon, R. M. and Verenikina, I. T. (2007). Towards Inclusive Schools: An Examination of Sociocultural Theory and Inclusive Practices and Policy in NSW DET Schools, *Learning and Socio-cultural Theory: Exploring Modern Vygotskian Perspectives International Workshop*, 1(1), 192-208. Retrieved from http://ro.uow.edu.au/cgi/viewcontent.cgi?article=1012&context=llrg
European Agency for Special Needs and Inclusive Education. (n.d). *Development of inclusion – Germany*. Retrieved from https://www.european-agency.org/country-information/germany/national-overview/development-of-inclusion
Evans, L (2007). *Inclusion*. Great Britain: Taylor and Francis.

Fan, M. (2004). *The idea of Integrated Education*. Georgia, United States of America: Valdosta State University.
Forbes, F. (2007). Inclusion Policy Towards Inclusion: an Australian Perspective. *Support for Learning*. 22(2), 66-71. Retrieved from http://www.waespaa.com.au/pdf/SupportForLearning-FionaForbes.pdf
Foreman, P. (2005). *Inclusion in action*. South Victoria, Australia: Thomson.

Friere, P. (1972). *Pedagogy of the Oppressed*. London: Penguin.

Gardiner, H. (1983). Frames of Mind: The Theory of Multiple Intelligences. London: Penguin.

Harman, B. (2002). *Inclusion/Integration: is there a difference?*. Retrieved from http://www.cdss.ca/images/pdf/general_information/integration_vs_inclusion.pdf
International Classification of Functioning, Disability and Health. Retrieved from http://www.who.int/classifications/icf/en/
James, A. (2010) *School Bullying*. Retrieved from http://www.nspcc.org.uk/inform/research/briefings/school_bullying_pdf_wdf73502.pdf
Jones, M, M. & McLean, K. J. (2012). Personalising Learning in Teacher Education through the use of Technology, *Australian Journal of Teacher Education*, 37 (1), 75-92. Retrieved from http://ro.ecu.edu.au/cgi/viewcontent.cgi?article=1604&context=ajte
Keegan, S. (2008). The SAGE Encyclopedia of Qualitative Research Methods. Given, L. http://dx.doi.org.ezproxy.une.edu.au/10.4135/9781412963909.n318
Kerridge, G. (2008). *Learning Disability*. Retrieved from http://www.newcastle.edu.au/Resources/Divisions/Services/Student%20and%20Academic%20Services/Student%20Support/NDCO/NDCO_eZine_Aut08.pdf

Klemm, K. (2009). Effective Investment in Education, Exceptionalism Special Schools: a study on the issues and effectiveness of Special Schools in Germany. Gutersloh, Germany: Bertelsmann Foundation. Retrieved from http://translate.google.com/translate?depth=1&hl=en&prev=/search%3Fq%3Dinklusion%2Bin%2Bgerman%2Bschule%26biw%3D1243%26bih%3D609&rurl=translate.google.com.au&sl=de&u=http://www.bertelsmann-stiftung.de/cps/rde/xbcr/SID-CFD0B446-AC96034A/bst/Foerderschule.pdf

Klemm, K. (2012). *Information for Teachers and visiting Teachers, Inclusion: School for all shapes.* Bonn, Germany: Aktion Mensch eV. Retrieved from http://translate.google.com.au/translate?hl=en&sl=de&u=http://publikationen.aktion-mensch.de/unterricht/Aktion-Mensch_Inklusion_Praxisheft.pdf&prev=/search%3Fq%3DDefinition%2Bf%25C3%25BCr%2BInklusion%26biw%3D1245%26bih%3D595

Leavitt, M. (2006). Team Teaching: Benefits and Challenges, *Speaking of Teaching*, 16 (1), 1-4. Retrieved from http://www.stanford.edu/dept/CTL/Newsletter/teamteaching.pdf

Longhurst, R. (2010). *Semi-structured Interviews and Focus Groups.* Book is called: Key Methods in Geography. Nicholas Clifford, Shaun French & Gill Valentine. SAGE Publications.

Montessori Australia. (n.d) *Montessori Approach.* Retrieved from http://montessori.org.au/montessori/approach.htm

Montessori, M. (2013). *The Montessori Method.* New Jersey: Transaction Publishers.

McCrady, B. S., Ladd, B., Vermont, L. and Steele, J. (2010). *Interviews in Addiction Research Methods.* Oxford, UK: Wiley-Blackwell.

Nes, F.V., Abma, T., Jonsson, H. & Deeg, D. (2010). Language differences in qualitative research: is meaning lost in translation?, *European Journal of Ageing*, 7 (4), 313-316. Retrieved from http://www.ncbi.nlm.nih.gov/pmc/articles/PMC2995873/

NSW Board of Studies. (2002) *.K-10 Curriculum Framework.* Retrieved from http://www.boardofstudies.nsw.edu.au/manuals/pdf_doc/curriculum_fw_K10.pdf

NSW Department of Education and Communities. (n.d). *The School Counseling Workforce in NSW Government Schools.* Retrieved from https://www.det.nsw.edu.au/media/downloads/about-us/statistics-and-research/public-reviews-and-enquiries/school-counselling-services-review/paper1-tscwings.pdf

Opdenakker, R. (2006). Advantages and Disadvantages of Four Interview Techniques in Qualitative Research [44 paragraphs]. *Forum Qualitative Sozialforschung / Forum: Qualitative Social Research*, 7(4), Art. 11, http://nbn-resolving.de/urn:nbn:de:0114-fqs0604118.

Pink, S. (2007). *Doing Visual Ethnography.* London: SAGE Publications.

Roulston, K. (2012). *Reflective Interviewing: A Guide to Theory and Practice.* University of Georgia, USA: Sage Publications.

Rule, P. (2010). *Bakhtin and Friere: Dialogue, dialetic and boundary learning.* Educational Philosophy and Theory. DOI: 10.1111/j.1469-5812.2009.00606.x

Russ-Eft, D. & Preskill, H. (2009). Evaluation in Organizations: A Systematic Approach to Enhancing Learning, Performance, and Change. New York: Basic Books.

Urbis. (2011). Literature Review on Meeting: The Psychological and Emotional wellbeing needs of Children and Young People: Models of Effective Practice in Educational Settings. Retrieved from https://www.det.nsw.edu.au/media/downloads/about-us/statistics-and-research/public-reviews-and-enquiries/school-counselling-services-review/models-of-effective-practice.pdf

Hanna Middendorf and Ingrid Harrington
5 An Exploration of how Inclusive Practices in Schools Influence Student Behaviour

5.1 Abstract

In 2009 the *UN Convention on the Rights of Persons with Disabilities* was ratified in Germany. Whilst the shift towards promoting an inclusive 'school for all' brought Germany in line with the global trend, it also presented a number of challenges for the German education system (Aktion Mensch e.V. 2013; 12).
In 1980, Australia began to discuss how an inclusive school system would make schools accessible for all children (NSW Auditor-General's Report 2006; 4), and to-date, all schools in Australia promote fully inclusive practices. Australia therefore was a logical choice to conduct a study into the impact of inclusion in schools. This study had a specific focus of how an inclusive school system may influence the social behaviours of students. Another aim of the study was to explore teacher perspectives on the amount of support offered to students with special needs, and to study the teacher's levels of confidence in promoting this.
The development of social skills is a complex process and having a focus on positive student social behaviour in schools maybe useful to conclude if an inclusive school setting promotes this.

5.2 . Literature Review

Literature suggests that children display appropriate social behaviour when they experience positive and friendly relationships with their peers (Forbes 2007; Gilmore 2010). Children with special needs seem to experience more difficulty when trying to initiate contact to other children (Forbes 2007; Gilmore 2010). Furthermore, these children feel socially excluded by other children (Forbes 2007). These are indicators that the self-perception of children with special needs may not always positive (Wekenmann and Schlottke 2001 p. 11).
    As the Australian Education system is fully inclusive, how their special needs are met in the classroom, and how their peers respond to this, will be a useful starting point from where to analyse the research findings. In the last decade, the

number of diagnoses of children with disabilities has increased, which can be attributed to better and more differentiated diagnoses thanks to medical advancements (cf. Gilmore, 2010). Another consideration of this research concerns the different types and manifestations of a 'Special Need' (NSW Education and Communities 2013). It is therefore possible that a child diagnosed with dyslexia, does not necessarily mean they also have difficulties engaging in the social curriculum of school. Current literature states that most children have some sort of special need if they are physically or intellectually disabled (Gilmore 2010). Research by (Schmitman gen. Pothmann 2010 p. 17) report that a friendly and respectful relationship between children and adults promote appropriate social behaviour, as students experience appreciation and recognition. Therefore, it is not unusual that students with special needs generally have good social skills, but are lacking only in certain other areas.

The Australian curriculum is oriented towards the harnessing resources and skills to meet the diverse needs of all students. By focusing on the inclusive school system in Australia, one can argue it should be possible to support all students, because the basic guideline of inclusion is to adapt the conditions to the needs and skills of all students (Schumann p. 2009). Should a student with special needs be greater than others, an academic, social and/or behavioural plan is collaboratively designed by the teacher, support teacher, and others involved with the student's welfare (NSW Education and Communities 2013). This individual plan is designed to accommodate the student's needs, identify the resources required, and build upon the student's abilities. The individual plans thereby facilitate how all students could feel supported, respected and appreciated by the school. Forbes (2007) states however, that a school system is only fully developed when the curriculum does not need to be adapted to children with special needs – "a successful school system is only achieved when the curriculum already is adapted to all children and their skills, resources and needs" (Forbes 2007 p. 66).

5.3 Collecting and Description of the Sample

The data was collected from two Australian Primary schools in Armidale, New South Wales (NSW). The two schools catered for students that typically experienced a low socio-economic status, and whose parents identified as Aboriginal or to another cultural ethnic background than Australian. Both schools were small in size reporting student populations of no more than 150 each. Due to the unique student profile, both schools regularly participated in collaborative research conducted by UNE academics and the Department of Education and Communities. Students in the final two years of Primary School (years five and six) aged between 10 and 12 years were asked to participate in a questionnaire due to the reading and comprehension ability needed to understand the questions. The questionnaire was distributed to two student classes totalling 33 students, of which 16 had been diagnosed with special needs, and 17 reported not having any special needs.

A total of 19 teachers from Schools A and B were interviewed and asked to share their views on how student social behaviour was influenced by the school-wide inclusive policy at their school. Semi-structured interviews were held with the teachers and recorded on site.

Prior to distributing the questionnaire to the students, the researcher sat in the classes to gain a sense of how the class proceeded each day, and for the students to become remotely familiar with the researcher's presence. Gathering data from both students and their teachers encouraged a balanced data set as students could answer how socially included they felt at school, and the teachers could comment on their observations of how students interacted throughout the school day.

5.3.1 Construction of the Questionnaire

The choice of a questionnaire as the student data collection tool was the correct instrument to use as it promoted anonymity that assured students of their privacy and confidentiality being upheld. This assurance may also have influenced students to respond more truthfully to the questionnaire questions, as they could take their time in responding without being questioned by the researcher in an interview situation.

The structure of the questionnaire had five categories, namely:
Socialisation of Students: Students were asked with whom and when they socialized with other students.
Negative School Experiences: Students were asked about possible sources of negative school experiences such as poor academic grades.

Problem and Conflict Resolution: Students were asked to comment about the process they use to respond and deal with issues and school-based conflict.

Parents and Teachers: Students were asked to comment whether their teacher and parents played a supportive or obstructive role in their engagement with school.

Student Attitudes Towards School and Free Time: Students were asked whether they enjoyed attending and engaging in the school day.

The different category questions were not grouped, but listed randomly in the questionnaire to reduce the chance of student bias in their responses. Two identical versions (A and B) of the questionnaire were circulated, with Version A going to students without special needs, and Version B going to students with special needs. This distribution assisted the data analysis for contrast, content and difference. No such differentiation was necessary for teachers. The questionnaires began by asking simple and uncomplicated questions. The first question concerned their age and number of siblings, followed by a question about their general view of school. The teachers' questionnaire began by asking about the number of students they taught in their class, and how many years of teaching experience they had. They were then asked to comment about what it was like for them to work at the school.

5.4 Results

5.4.1 Socialisation of Students

No overt differences were recorded between the two cohorts of students with and without special needs in this category. Of the 33 students that participated in the questionnaire, 19 without special needs liked to play with a best friend during the break, and 11 with special needs with many other students. Of these 19 children 15, sometimes met up with fellow students out of school hours. Of the 11 children with special needs who liked to play with many other students, 7 sometimes met up with fellow students out of school hours.

Twenty-five students without special needs reported that they enjoyed being surrounded by many other people, and 14 of those said it was easy for them to get into contact with others. The results showed that 58% of students with special needs said it was not easy to get into contact with other people, whilst 42% of pupils without special needs said the same.

Students were asked if they sometimes did not want to play with other children, or if sometimes other children didn't want to play with them. The answers showed that 21 out of 33 students sometimes did not want to play with other children, and out these 21, 12 said that other children did not want to play with them. In summary, 17 students with special needs said that sometimes other children did not want to play with them.

Considering the responses, it can be seen that the students with special needs are relatively divided when it comes to wanting to play with other children when compared to those without special needs. Nine children with special needs sometimes did not want to play with other children and seven always wanted to. Out of these nine children, eight thought that other children sometimes did not want to play with them, and from the other seven, two said that sometimes they thought other children did not want to play with them. Conversely, 12 out of 17 children without special needs said that sometimes they did not want to play with other children. Eight students said that other children always wanted to play with them. In summary, 10 pupils without special needs said that other children always wanted to play with them.

Similarly, the children were asked about the nature of their contact with others in their free time at school. Ten of 33 students said they never met friends pursuing their preferred interest. 19 children sometimes pursued their preferred interest with other children, and four always met other children whilst pursuing their preferred interest. It is noteworthy that 41% of students without special needs did not meet other children, and 35% sometimes did. Approximately 19% of children with special needs never met other children whilst pursuing their preferred interest, and 81% sometimes did meet other children. Here, a difference between children with special needs and those without can be noted. The results show that children with special needs also socialise with others in their free time at school, whilst students without special needs reported spending less time with outers whilst pursuing their preferred interest.

Teachers were asked to comment on how they thought students with special needs interact with other students in school, and how these students reacted towards them. 15 of 19 teachers thought that students with special needs had an outgoing personality, and 10 of 19 teachers thought that other students found it easy to interact with the students with special needs. Differentiating the teachers' answers, 54.54% (n=11) of the teachers from School A, and 57.14% (n=8) of the teachers from School B thought that other students interacted well with the children with special needs.

The data concerning how students without special needs interact with children with special needs is equally inconclusive. Eleven of 19 teachers did not report a noticeable difference in student interaction. Six teachers from school A (n=12) did see a difference, and five (n=7) teachers from School B said they saw no difference.

5.4.2   Negative School Experiences

The results of how students viewed negative experiences and dealt with this is discussed in this section. 20 of 33 students noticed that others sometimes talked about them, and six were of the opinion that others always talked about them. 25 students (n=33) said that they did not get sad when they had a negative school experience. There was no difference between the results of children with and without special needs.

From the teachers' perspective, the students with special needs became easily discouraged if they received a bad grade. Twelve teachers (n=19) thought that this perspective was in part true, and two thought it was true. The results from School A reported that 12 of 10 teachers thought that children with special needs were more easily discouraged if they did not perform will in academic tasks, whereas teachers from School B were divided, as four teachers thought that children with special needs were more easily discouraged, and three said it was always the case.

5.4.3   Problem and Conflict Resolution

The results showed that 28 of the 33 students were happy to ask a teacher for help in resolving problems and conflict at school. Of the 19 teachers, 11 teachers thought that students with special needs did not actively seek help to resolve their conflict.

The results from both schools separately report that six of 11 teachers from School A said that students with special needs avoided conflict, and six of seven teachers from School B said the same thing.

5.4.4   Positive and Negative Influence by Parents and Teachers

Students were asked if they saw a difference in the way they were treated by teachers when compared to other students.

The results showed that 22 students without special needs (n=33) thought teachers treated everyone equally. Ten students with special needs felt that teachers treated them differently to other students, but were unable to say if the different treatment was positive or negative. A differentiated view of the student's answers shows that half the students without special needs saw a difference in the way the teachers treated their students. It is noteworthy that out of the other half who believed that teachers treated students equally, two thought that teachers did favour some students.

All teachers had said that they found it easy to teach their classes and 17 of 19 teachers thought they generated a positive classroom environment. The teachers made a number of comments regarding their perspectives of their student's parents. Ten of 19 teachers said that the parents of children with special needs would sometimes complain about an aspect of the school. Specifically, seven of the 12 teachers from School A did not think the parents would complain, whilst five of seven teachers from School B thought that parents of children with special needs would complain more often.

Furthermore, 13 of 19 teachers were of the opinion that the parents of children with special needs had higher expectations for their lessons. There is no significant difference between the answers of the teachers from both schools. Similarly, 14 teachers (n=19) said that parents liked to attend school field trips. Again, there was no real difference between the answers from the teachers from both schools.

5.4.5 Student Attitudes towards School and Free Time

Students were asked if they liked attending school of which 25 of 33 said they did, yet all 33 students said they looked forward to the school recess breaks. The results reported eight negative answers were given by three students without special needs (n=17), and five with special needs (n=16).

The responses to this category show that students with and without special needs had attended more than one school between one and five times. Eight of the 17 students without special needs had never changed schools, whilst seven of 16 students with special needs had never changed schools.
Most students (31 of 33) reported that they pursued a hobby in their spare time. The Table below reflects how all students spent their spare time:

	Playing Sport	IT/Digital media	Meet with friends	Spend time with family	Spend time outdoors
Students with Special Needs	81%	100%	12.5%	5%	12.5%
Students without Special Needs	76.5%	23.5%	6%	12.5%	17.6%

Tabelle 5-1

Of the 19 teachers from Schools A and B, nine were of the opinion that students with special needs disrupt the lessons, whilst 10 did not share this opinion. A difference between the schools can be seen, as 58% of teachers from School A, and 71% of teachers from School B said that students with special needs did not disrupt the lessons. Of these 10 teachers, six said that students with special needs were more dedicated when it came to extracurricular activities. 50% of teachers from school A and 28.57% of teachers from School B thought that children with special needs were more dedicated when it came to extracurricular activities.

5.5 Discussion

Research by Caldarella and Merrell (1997) outlines five domains of social skills that will be used to contextualise the analysis of this research. Their five domains are:
1. *Peer Relationships*: All children have social contact to peers, as well in school as in their free time. However, it may not easy for children with special needs to make new acquaintances than for those without special needs.
2. *Self-Management*: Students do not withdraw in conflict situations and are not discouraged by school-based failures. The research claims that students with special needs are more easily discouraged by bad grades, but the students themselves disagree.
3. *Academic*: The teachers from Schools A and B thought that students with special needs tended to disturb lessons more, and they had more commitment when it came to extracurricular activities.
4. *Compliance*: Students like the company of others and sometimes pursue their hobby and/or interests with other students, which is indicative of a certain level of cooperation and adaptability.
5. *Assertion*: Children with special needs did not avoid conflict, which showed they stood up for themselves. Despite showing initiative and participating in activities, they still reported difficulty making new friends (Caldarella and Merrell 1997 p. 245).

5.5.1 Social Inclusion

Both the teacher and student results show that all students are socially included. This is supported by the fact that some students socialize during and outside of school time. Despite being socially included, the children with special needs reported some difficulties getting to know other children, feeling that some other students did not want to play with them. This is in contrast to the responses from students without special needs that said it was easy for them to get to know other children, yet they preferred to spend time alone during school time.

Interesting parallels can be drawn from the two cohorts of students on this point: whilst students with special needs want to play with other students, other students do not want this. Whilst other students want to play with children without special needs, more often, these students do not want this.

More than half the teachers from the combined teacher cohort said that children without special needs did not behave differently when they were in contact with children with special needs. This indicates that students at both schools behave respectfully towards each other. Therefore, the conclusion can be drawn that children with special needs have an equally well-developed social network as children without special needs.

5.5.2 Negative Experiences

All students sampled reported that they thought that other students spoke about them to other students, albeit positive and/or negatively.

The results also reported that all students said they had not experienced any sort of school-based failure, but said if they had, they would be able to manage it. It is possible however, that the students did not answer truthfully because they did not want to admit their own weaknesses to themselves or the interviewer. Teachers stated that students with special needs had a lower tolerance for school-based failures, possibly because they shared a perception that they viewed students with special needs as being more vulnerable.

5.5.3 Problem and Conflict Solving

All students were comfortable in asking teachers for help when faced with a problem. This shows that the students can advocate for themselves and have strategies on how to deal with conflict and challenging situations.

The teacher responses confirm that students are able to advocate and ask for support from others. This refutes the earlier teacher perception that children with special needs are more vulnerable. The responses however, do not indicate if the student response in the conflict situations was appropriate.

An indication whether the student's strategies were appropriate may be provided by responses to the category about the positive and/or negative influences of parents and teachers. It may be assumed that if parents were positive role-models to their children, then it may be assumed that they have better-prepared their children with different and appropriate strategies in response to conflict.

5.5.4 Positive or Negative Influence of Parents and Teachers

The students reported that their teacher had a positive and respectful influence on them in class. However, over half of the students surveyed with special needs were of the opinion that their teacher favoured other students and were not always respectful. The responses from the children without special needs confirms this. Some responses from the teachers reflected that they believed that some teachers lacked the professional confidence and competence to effectively deal with students with special needs.

The data reports that the parents have a positive and negative influence on their children. According to the teachers, the positive influence can be seen in that parents of children with special needs have higher expectations for their children in the class room lessons.

5.5.5 Attitude towards School and Free Time

The students' attitudes towards school can be described as generally positive. Almost all children like going to school and look forward to the breaks. Considering these results, one can form the hypothesis that the teachers succeed in creating a respectful and comfortable atmosphere. Furthermore, it can be assumed that the students behave in a way that is respectful towards the teacher and each other, and their behaviour is not characterised by inappropriate behaviour or aggression.

More that half of the students had only attended one school. This supports the view that the students and their parents are satisfied with the influence the school has on their child. The questionnaire did not ask to elaborate on why a student had changed schools, and this aspect could be researched further.

The teacher's answers do not show clearly if children with special needs negatively disrupt the lessons because the teachers from both schools gave similar opinions. More research would need to be conducted to gain a clearer position on this question.

Teachers from Schools A and B reported that students without special needs did not show more commitment to their studies, yet they thought that students with special needs did show more commitment to their studies. Therefore, it would be necessary to expand the sample or take another survey with more participants.

The data reporting leisure time behaviour allowed for distinguishing between six categories of activities. Just as many students with special needs like to play sports as students without special needs. It is noteworthy that many students engaged with digital media, but children without special needs seldom did. Most students said that they met other students in their free time, hence the conclusion that students with special needs withdraw from social contacts during their free time cannot be drawn.

5.6 Limitations of the Study

This chapter explored the impact a 'whole-school' approach to inclusion had upon the students at Schools A and B in Armidale, NSW, Australia. Some limitations of the study include that as the sample size was too small, no true conclusions can be drawn and viewed as representative.

A number of the questionnaire questions need to be revised to have more differentiated answers that could provide greater insight into student behaviour.

The teachers' questionnaire could have also contained more specific questions about the behaviour of students without special needs, as the research primarily focused only on the behaviours of children with special needs. Research that is concerned with inclusive school systems should consider all participants equally because every opinion has valuable views and provides a more accurate, representative picture.

An opportunity for students and teachers to elaborate on the positive and/or negative behaviours that impact on a student's social behaviour could be provided so as to identify where specific concerns lay. This may be helpful for the development and design of an inclusive system in the current German education system so as to promote a successful inclusive education system.

5.7 Conclusion

The Australian education system is inclusive, progressive and implemented well. However, a question remains that how inclusive is the system really when the curriculum still needs to be adapted to meet the needs, resources and skills of children with special needs. The aspiration of an inclusive school system should be that the curriculum incorporates the skills, resources and needs of all children from the start and does not need to be adapted. A closer understanding of the Australian education system will show that whilst the learning outcomes remain the same, the pedagogy and resources adopted may differ to meet the varying needs of all students.

5.8 References:

AIHW (Australian Institute of Health and Welfare) (2015). *Disability support services: services provided under the National Disability Agreement 2013-14*. Bulletin no. 30. Cat. no. AUS 192. Canberra: AIHW.

Aktion Mensch e.V. (Hrsg.) (2013) Ein großer Schritt nach vorn. Das Übereinkommen der Vereinten Nationen über die Rechte von Menschen mit Behinderung. Mainz (AG Mainz) http://publikationen.aktion-mensch.de/5mai/AktionMensch_5Mai_UN-Konvention.pdf (24.07.2013)

Caldarella, P. , Merell, K. W. (1997). Common dimensions of social skills of children and adolescents: A taxonomy of positive behaviours. In: School Psychology Review, 26, 244 – 264

Crick, N. R. , Dodge, K. A. (1994). A review and reformation of social information-processing mechanisms in children's social adjustment. In: Psychological Bulletin, 115, 74 – 101

Forbes, F. (2007). Towards inclusion. An Australian perspective. In: Support for Learning. Volume 22, Nr. 2

Gilmore, H. (2010). Teachers overwhelmed by special needs. In: Pressemitteilung. http://www.smh.com.au/national/education/teachers-overwhelmed-by-   special-needs-20100720-10jjh.html (20.06.2013)

NSW Auditor-General's Report (2006). Educating Primary School Students with Disabilities. In: Performance Audit, NSW Department of Education

Schmitman gen. Pothmann, M. (2010). Kinder brauchen Freunde – Soziale Fertigkeiten fördern. Gruppentherapie bei AD(H)S und anderen Verhaltensauffälligkeiten. Stuttgart (Klett-Cotta)

Schumann, B. (2009). Inklusion statt Integration – eine Verpflichtung zum Systemwechsel. Deutsche Schulverhältnisse auf dem Prüfstand des Völkerrechts, in: Sonderdruck Pädagogik, Heft 2 http://www.gew.de/Binaries/Binary43645/SonderdruckManifest.pdf(24.07.2013)

Wekenmann, S. B. / Schlottke, P. F. (2001). Soziale Situationen meistern. Ein störungsübergreifendes Gruppentraining für Kinder. Göttingen (Hogrefe)

Katharina Steinbeck
6 Inklusive Schulen - Inklusive Lehrkräfte?
Wie viel Sonderpädagogik braucht das Lehramtsstudium, damit Lehrkräfte auch für inklusive Schulsysteme ausgebildet sind?

Ein qualitatives Forschungsprojekt zur Ausbildung von Lehrkräften an inklusiven Schulen in Armidale, Australien.

6.1 Zusammenfassung

Mit der Ratifizierung der UN-Konvention über die Rechte der Menschen mit Behinderung wurde der Grundstein zur Umstellung auf ein inklusives Bildungssystem in Deutschland gelegt. Fachliche Diskussionen zeigen, dass Lehrkräfte in Deutschland während ihres Lehramtsstudiums nicht genügend Vorbereitung in den Bereichen Sonderpädagogik und Inklusion erhalten, um den Anforderungen des inklusiven Klassenzimmers gerecht zu werden. Das Forschungsprojekt untersucht, ob Lehrkräfte, die in Australien in inklusiven Schulsettings arbeiten, auf ihre Tätigkeit vorbereitet wurden und welche Empfehlungen sie für den Aufbau des Lehramtsstudiums aussprechen. Die Ergebnisse, welche aufzeigen, dass nicht ausreichend Vorbereitung auf die Lehrtätigkeit in inklusiven Schulen gegeben ist, lassen sich auf das Deutsche System übertragen und es kristallisiert sich heraus, dass die Ausbildung von inklusiven Lehrkräften theoretische und praktische Erfahrungen mit heterogenen Lerngruppen und sonderpädagogischen Themen beinhalten muss.

Schlüsselwörter: Lehrkräfte, Inklusion, inklusive Schulen, Lehramtsstudium, Vorbereitung, Sonderpädagogik

6.2 Inklusive Schulen in Deutschland und ihre Herausforderungen

Seit der Ratifizierung der UN-Konvention über die Rechte der Menschen mit Behinderung durch Deutschland im Jahr 2009 ist die Bundesrepublik verpflichtet, Menschen mit Behinderungen in allen Lebensbereichen eine gleichberechtigte und selbstbestimmte Lebensführung zu ermöglichen. Dies schließt auch das Recht auf Bildung mit ein, welches in Artikel 24 der Konvention festgehalten wird. Wie schwer sich Deutschland trotz Ratifizierung mit der Umsetzung der Konvention tut, wird deutlich, wenn man sich die deutsche Übersetzung anschaut. Während es im englischen Originaltext heißt: „ (...) States Parties shall ensure an *inclusive* (Hervorh. d. Verf.) education system at all levels and life long learning (...)", heißt es in der deutschen Übersetzung: „gewährleisten die Vertragsstaaten ein *integratives* (Hervorh. d. Verf.) Bildungssystem auf allen Ebenen und lebenslanges Lernen (...)". Bereits durch diese Übersetzung wird deutlich, wie sehr die Tradition des Bildungssystems in Deutschland von Selektion geprägt ist. Eine integrative Bildungslandschaft würde bedeuten, dass sich Kinder mit Behinderungen in die Regelschulen integrieren sollen (Reich 2012, S. 36). Im Gegensatz hierzu müsste eine inklusive Schule so ausgestattet sein, dass sie jede Schülerin und jeden Schüler als gleichberechtigtes Individuum aufnehmen und unterrichten kann (und muss), die Grundlagen hierfür müssen von staatlicher Seite erbracht werden (ebd.). Hinz weist darauf hin, dass seit 2000 die Diskussion um das Verhältnis von Integration zu Inklusion anhält, da dieses Verhältnis vom Verständnis der einzelnen Begriffe abhängt. So kann auch ein bestimmtes Verständnis von Integration eine umfassende, im Sinne von keinen Menschen ausschließende, Integration meinen (Hinz 2012, S. 40ff.).

Die erste große Herausforderung für Deutschland besteht darin, die Bildungslandschaft neu zu strukturieren, weg von einem selektierenden hin zu einem inklusiven System. Dies erschließt sich aus Absatz 2 des Artikels 24 der UN-Konvention über die Rechte der Menschen mit Behinderung, nach dem Menschen mit Behinderungen nicht vom unentgeltlichen Regelschulsystem ausgeschlossen werden dürfen. Die *Schule für alle* beinhaltet aber mehr als die formelle Öffnung der Regelschule für Schülerinnen und Schüler mit Behinderung durch die Eingliederung von Sonderpädagogik in die ansonsten unveränderte Praxis des Schulsystems (Seitz 2011, S. 2). Inklusion bedeutet, Diversitäten nicht nur zu akzeptieren, sondern wertzuschätzen und Heterogenität als Ressource anzuerkennen. Grundlage für die Umsetzung von Inklusion im Bildungssystem ist es jedoch, dass die Gesellschaft im Generellen ein inklusives Menschen- und Weltbild internalisiert, denn Inklusion im Klassenraum bringt wenig, wenn die Mitglieder einer Gesellschaft diskriminierende und ausschließende Normen weiterleben. Es geht also um eine grundlegende Haltung, ohne die Inklusion nicht gelingen kann.

Eine weitere Herausforderung für Deutschland bei der Umstellung auf ein inklusives Bildungssystem besteht darin, dass die Zuständigkeit für den Bereich Bildung durch die Föderalismusreform I vom 1. September 2006 von Bundesebene auf Landesebene übertragen wurde (Patt 2012, S. 205). Durch diese Entscheidungsmacht der einzelnen Bundesländer bestehen momentan große Unterschiede hinsichtlich des Fortschritts und der Methode der Einführung inklusiver Bildungseinrichtungen (hierzu Schlamp und Schlamp-Diekmann 2013, S. 18ff.). Bildungsgerechtigkeit kann aber nur entstehen, wenn alle Lernenden die gleichen

Voraussetzungen und Rechte beim Zugang zu Bildung haben, unabhängig von ihrem Wohnort.
Ebenfalls entscheidend bei der Umstellung auf ein inklusives Bildungssystem ist die Frage, welche Professionen welche Aufgaben übernehmen. Die Eingliederung von Sonderpädagoginnen und Sonderpädagogen in die Regelschule mit dem Auftrag, lediglich die Kinder mit diagnostiziertem besonderem Förderbedarf auch besonders zu fördern, kann dem Grundgedanken von Inklusion nicht gerecht werden, da in diesem Falle wieder separiert würde und der Unterrichtsalltag darauf hinaus liefe, dass Schülerinnen und Schüler mit sonderpädagogischem Förderbedarf von den Fachkräften der Sonderpädagogik und Regelschüler von Regellehrkräften gefördert würden. Unbestritten ist, dass interdisziplinäre Zusammenarbeit wichtig ist; die Modelle von Zusammenarbeit der Professionen Regellehramt und Sonderpädagogik sind vielfältig. Will man der Konvention jedoch gerecht werden, so müssen alle Lehrämter inklusive Bildung als Thema integrieren (Moser/ Demmer-Diekmann 2013, S. 155). Auch Heinrich et al. kommen zu dem Entschluss, „dass eine umfassende sonderpädagogische Vorstellung von Inklusion über Individualisierung dem Grundgedanken der UN-Behindertenrechtskonvention viel stärker entspricht als eine strikte Arbeitsteilung zwischen pädagogischer Aufgabe einerseits und psychologisch bzw. medizinisch-therapeutischer andererseits" (Heinrich/ Urban/ Werning 2013: 78) und plädieren aus diesem Grund für den Ausbau des sonderpädagogischen Wissens der Regellehrkräfte und des fachlichen Wissens der Sonderpädagoginnen und Sonderpädagogen (ebd., S.108).

6.3 Die Herausforderungen der Lehrkraft an inklusiven Schulen und ihre Konsequenzen

Um inklusive Bildung zu ermöglichen, sind die Lehrkräfte, die in diesem System arbeiten (oder arbeiten sollen) wichtigstes Element, da sie das System Schule tragen. Eine inklusive Schule kann demnach nur so gut sein, wie ihre Lehrkräfte es sind.
Nach Wocken bedeutet inklusiver Unterricht, „dass alle Kinder einer unausgelesenen und ungeteilten Gruppe sich allgemeine Bildung nach individuellem Vermögen und individuellen Bedürfnissen in vielfältigen Lernprozessen mit gemeinsamen und differenziellen Lernsituationen unter Nutzung förderlicher Ressourcen ohne behindernde Lernbarrieren und ohne diskriminierende und exkludierende Praxen sowie mit entwicklungsorientierter Lernevaluationaneignen können, und zwar mit aktiver Unterstützung von kooperierenden Pädagogen und sozialen Netzwerken." (Wocken 2011, S. 134).

Doch wie kann eine Lehrkraft einen solchen Unterricht stemmen? Damit inklusiver Unterricht erfolgreich sein kann, ist es wichtig, dass die Lehrkraft im inklusiven System bestimmte Werte verinnerlicht, die für sie handlungsleitend sind. Die European Agency hat in ihrem Profil für inklusive Lehrkräfte verschiedene Werte festgehalten. Ein Grundbaustein besteht darin, die Diversität der Lernenden zu wertschätzen, indem Unterschiede als Ressourcen wahrgenommen werden, die die Bildung aller fördern. Außerdem unterstützt eine inklusive Lehrkraft alle Lernenden, indem sie das schulische, emotionale, soziale und praktische Lernen aller, durch effiziente Unterrichtsansätze für heterogene Klassen fördert. Hinzu kommt die Zusammenarbeit mit Eltern, Familien und anderen Fachkräften aus dem Bildungsbereich. Letzter Punkt des Profils für inklusive Lehrkräfte ist die Übernahme von der Verantwortung für das eigene lebenslange Lernen durch kontinuierliche berufliche Weiterbildung (European Agency 2012, S. 13ff.).

Im Zuge der Umstellung auf ein inklusives Bildungssystem verändert sich auch die Rolle der Lehrkraft: ist diese in der Regelklasse Hauptdarstellerin oder Hauptdarsteller des Unterrichtsgeschehens, so definiert sie sich im inklusiven Klassenzimmer als Beraterin oder Berater und Begleiterin oder Begleiter der Lernenden (Scholz 2012b, S. 39). Scholz verdeutlicht, dass die Umstellung auf inklusiven Unterricht nicht nur neue Herausforderungen bereit hält sondern auch neue Chancen und Möglichkeiten aufbringt: Da die Lehrkraft im inklusiven System die Verantwortung des Lernens in einem größeren Umfang an die Lernenden abgibt, entsteht eine neue Struktur des Unterrichts. Die Lehrkraft ist dafür zuständig, die Lernumgebung für eine heterogene Lerngruppe adäquat zu gestalten und zu strukturieren. Neben den Rahmenbedingungen, die die Lehrkraft herstellt, können und sollen die Lernenden in die Planung und Durchführung des Unterrichts einbezogen werden. Als Voraussetzung für ein Gelingen hierfür benennt er eine veränderte Grundhaltung der Lehrkraft, die ihren Blick auf Heterogenität schärft und Unterschiede innerhalb der Lerngruppe erkennt und akzeptiert, ebenso wie die Förderung einer Vertrauenskultur, in der die Lehrperson darauf vertraut, „dass jeder Schüler lernen will und selbständig zu sinnvollen Konstruktionen gelangt" (ebd., S.42).

Seitz betont ebenfalls, dass inklusiver Unterricht nicht darin besteht, einen Lehrplan für Regelschülerinnen und -schüler zu entwickeln und dann den Versuch zu starten, Schülerinnen und Schüler mit besonderen Bedürfnissen in diesen Lehrplan zu integrieren, sondern individualisierten Unterricht für die gesamte Lerngruppe aus der Perspektive der Lernenden zu gestalten (Seitz 2011, S. 2f.). Die Heterogenität muss hierbei ganz klar als Ressource verstanden werden, die den Lernprozess aller voranbringt. Sawalies et al benennen als Anforderungen an Lehrpersonen in inklusiven Schulen neben dem Verständnis von Inklusion als gesellschaftliches Anliegen und den Grundlagen individueller Förderung außerdem differenzierte diagnostische Kompetenzen, Klassenführungskompetenzen, die Fähigkeit zur Teamarbeit und Schul-, Organisations- und Unterrichtsentwicklung sowie beraterische Kompetenzen (Sawalies et al 2013, S. 4f.).

Die veränderte Rolle der Lehrkraft im inklusiven Klassenzimmer und das neue Grundverständnis vom Lernprozess in heterogenen Lerngruppen zieht die Konsequenz nach sich, dass die Ausbildung von angehenden Lehrpersonen ebenfalls einer Veränderung bedarf, damit sie den Anforderungen der neuen Lernumgebung und Lernstruktur gerecht werden können. Sowohl das Verständnis für Inklusion und inklusive Prozesse als auch die Kompetenzen, die benötigt werden, um inklusive Strukturen zu fördern, müssen erlernt werden.

Dies ist auch in der UN-Konvention über die Rechte der Menschen mit Behinderung festgehalten. So heißt es in Artikel 24 Absatz 4:

„Um zur Verwirklichung dieses Rechts beizutragen, treffen die Vertragsstaaten geeignete Maßnahmen zur Einstellung von Lehrkräften, einschließlich solcher mit Behinderungen, die in Gebärdensprache oder Brailleschrift ausgebildet sind, und zur Schulung von Fachkräften sowie Mitarbeitern und Mitarbeiterinnen auf allen Ebenen des Bildungswesens. Diese Schulung schließt die Schärfung des Bewusstseins für Behinderungen und die Verwendung geeigneter ergänzender und alternativer Formen, Mittel und Formate der Kommunikation sowie pädagogische Verfahren und Materialien zur Unterstützung von Menschen mit Behinderungen ein.".

Die Kultusministerkonferenz hält 2011 hierzu fest, dass die Länder die Vorbereitung auf ein inklusives System von Lehrkräften aller Schularten in Aus-, Fort- und Weiterbildung gewährleisten (Kultusministerkonferenz 2011, S. 20).

An dieser Stelle wird wieder deutlich, welche Auswirkungen das föderale System im Bereich Bildung für Deutschland hat: die Aufgabe der Länder ist zwar offiziell festgehalten, auf welche Art und Weise dies geschieht, darf (und muss) das jeweilige Land jedoch selber entscheiden, sodass die Initiativen zur Professionalisierung der Lehrkräfte für inklusive Systeme zwischen den Bundesländern sehr unter unterschiedlich sind (Hillenbrand/ Melzer/ Hagen 2013, S. 37ff.).

Um festzustellen, welche Kompetenzen Studierende während des Lehramtsstudiums für die Tätigkeit in inklusiven Schulsystemen vermittelt bekommen sollten, ist es interessant seinen Blick auf die Lehrpersonen zu wenden, die bereits in einem solchen System tätig sind. Ausgehend von dem Wissen, dass in New South Wales, Australien Schulen schon seit mehreren Jahren inklusiv arbeiten, wurde ein Forschungsprojekt initiiert, bei dem australische Lehrkräfte zu ihrer Vorbereitung auf inklusive Strukturen befragt wurden. Das Vorhaben besteht darin, zu untersuchen, ob und wie die Lehrkräfte dort, also an Schulen, die bereits inklusiv arbeiten, auf ihre Tätigkeit vorbereitet wurden.

6.4 Das Forschungsprojekt: Lehrkräfte an inklusiven Schulen in Armidale, Australien

Forschungsfrage
Die Idee des Forschungsprojekts stammt aus Gesprächen mit deutschen Lehramtsstudentinnen und -studenten, bei welchen das Wort „Inklusion" allgemeines Unbehagen auslöste. Diesem Unbehagen liegt nach eigenen Aussagen das Gefühl der Überforderung zugrunde, da eine Vorbereitung auf inklusive Schulsysteme während des Studiums nicht gegeben ist. Wie aber kann ein inklusives Schulsystem funktionieren, wenn die Lehrkräfte, die es tragen, nicht adäquat auf ihre Arbeit vorbereitet werden?

Ausgehend von der Situation im deutschen Bildungssystem entstand die Überlegung, bereits inklusiv arbeitende Schulsysteme und ihre Lehrkräfte zu untersuchen. Forschungsfrage war hierbei, wieviel Sonderpädagogik das Lehramtsstudium benötigt, um Lehrkräfte für inklusive Schulsysteme vorzubereiten.

Datenerhebung und Auswertung
Die Interviews wurden an zwei Grundschulen (Primary Schools) in Armidale geführt. Die Schulen wurden durch Kontaktaufnahme von der Kooperationspartnerin in Armidale, Dr. Ingrid Harrington (University of New England UNE, New South Wales), angefragt, sodass sowohl die Schulleitung als auch die Lehrkräfte über das Forschungsprojekt informiert waren.

Insgesamt nahmen 14 Lehrkräfte an der qualitativen Befragung teil. An der ersten Schule wurden sechs Interviews geführt, alle mit weiblichen Lehrkräften. Die anderen acht Interviews wurden an der zweiten Schule geführt, sechs von ihnen mit weiblichen Lehrkräften und zwei mit männlichen. Der Anteil an weiblichen und männlichen Teilnehmern entsprach in etwa dem Anteil der weiblichen und männlichen Lehrkräfte an den Schulen insgesamt.

Die Auswahl der Probanden erfolgte zufällig: Lehrkräfte, die gerade einen Leerlauf und somit „Freizeit" hatten, wurden angesprochen und zur Teilnahme am Interview gebeten. Alle angesprochenen Lehrkräfte sagten der Teilnahme am Interview zu.
Die Interviews hatten im Durchschnitt eine Länge von zehn Minuten, das Kürzeste hatte eine Länge von sechs Minuten, das Längste dauerte 15 Minuten. Alle Interviews wurden elektronisch festgehalten.

Das gesammelte Material wurde wörtlich transkribiert und nach der qualitativen Inhaltsanalyse nach Mayring ausgewertet (hierzu Mayring 2010, S. 68f.).

6.5 Ergebnisse des Forschungsprojektes

Ausbildung der Lehrkräfte und Vorbereitung auf ein inklusives Schulsystem
Die 14 in Armidale befragten Lehrkräfte weisen verschiedene Qualifikationen für ihre Lehrtätigkeit aus: sechs Lehrkräfte haben einen Bachelor in Lehramt, zwei Lehrkräfte einen Bachelor in Grundschullehramt, eine Lehrkraft besitzt einen Bachelor in Grundschullehramt und einen Master in Inclusive Education, eine Lehrkraft hat einen Bachelor in Grundschullehramt und einen Bachelor in Sonderpädagogik, eine Lehrkraft einen Bachelor und ein Diplom in Lehramt, zwei Lehrkräfte besitzen einen Bachelor of Arts und ein Diplom in Lehramt und eine Lehrkraft („assistant") verfügt über eine Krankenschwesterausbildung.

Von den 14 befragten Lehrkräften haben neun in irgendeiner Form Veranstaltungen zum Thema Sonderpädagogik oder Inklusion besucht, fünf Personen hingegen hatten während ihres Studiums keinerlei Kontakt zu diesem Themenkreis. Was den Umfang und die Inhalte der besuchten Veranstaltungen angeht, zeigt sich bei den neun betroffenen Lehrkräften eine große Bandbreite: vier der neun Personen sprechen von einer Unit (Modul?), die sie über ein Semester oder über ein Jahr besucht haben und die Sonderpädagogik thematisierte. Drei dieser Lehrkräfte berichten von eher theoretischen und generellen Informationen, welche sie während dieser Sonderpädagogik-Unit erlernten und die sie als nicht besonders hilfreich einstufen. Nur eine dieser vier Lehrkräfte empfand die Lerneinheit zum Thema Sonderpädagogik und Inklusion als sehr hilfreich, da sie über den Umgang mit Verhaltensauffälligkeiten und sonderpädagogischen Förderbedarf/ besondere Bedürfnisse unterrichtet wurde und Methoden erlernen konnte, wie sie ihren Unterricht den verschiedenen Bedürfnissen der Kinder anpassen könne. Zwei weitere Lehrkräfte geben an, drei oder vier Units zum Themenkreis besucht zu haben, eine Lehrkraft berichtet von weniger speziellen, sondern generellen Informationen. Eine andere Lehrkraft jedoch erläutert, dass das Thema Sonderpädagogik und inklusiver Unterricht nicht nur während spezieller Units über das ganze Studium erlernt werden konnte, sondern außerdem in alle anderen Kurse eingebaut wurde. So wurde z.B. im Sportseminar durch praktische Übungen erfahren, wie man Sportunterricht so gestalten kann, dass Kinder mit Behinderungen eingebunden sind. Auffällig hierbei ist, dass diese Lehrkraft erst kürzlich ihr Studium abgeschlossen hat, was darauf schließen lassen lässt, dass Universitäten in Australien vermehrt die Themen Sonderpädagogik und inklusiver Unterricht in ihr Lehrprogramm aufnehmen. Die drei verbleibenden Lehrkräfte, die von sonderpädagogischen Inhalten während ihres Studiums sprechen, haben diese in Form eines gesonderten Studiums erlernt: zwei während des Bachelorstudiums der Sonderpädagogik und eine während des Masterstudiums „Inklusiver Unterricht" („Inclusive Education"). Letztere berichtet von wichtigen erlernten Kenntnissen:

„So, inclusive programming I passed a developing individual education with students. Looking at a range of things ranging from high disabilities, children with high disabilities right through down to children on the lower end of the spectrum so looking at all different sorts of disabilities particularly program was a big focus. And looking at policies, a big policy that focused on injury."

Die Lehrkräfte wurden weiterhin gefragt, ob sie sich auf die Arbeit mit Kindern mit sonderpädagogischem Förderbedarf/Behinderungen vorbereitet gefühlt haben, als sie ihre Stelle an einer inklusiven Schule angetreten haben. Nur vier der 14 befragten Personen bejahen dies, zehn Personen hingegen haben sich nicht vorbereitet gefühlt. Zwei dieser zehn Personen räumen ein, dass sie sich durch ein Praktikum in einer inklusiven Klasse bzw. in einer Förderklasse besser vorbereitet gefühlt haben. Wichtig hierbei ist, dass die vier Personen, die sich vorbereitet gefühlt haben, die Personen sind, welche Sonderpädagogik während eines extra Studiums oder in einem hohen und praktischen Ausmaß im Lehramtsstudium studiert haben. Dies lässt die Schlussfolgerung zu, dass eine Kombination aus einem regulären Lehramtsstudium und einem Sonderpädagogikstudium gute Voraussetzungen für Lehrkräfte inklusiver Schulen bietet.

Vorschläge für den Aufbau eines Lehramtsstudiums Der Schwerpunkt der vorliegenden Untersuchung lag darin herauszufinden, welche Studieninhalte Lehrkräfte, die bereits in einem inklusiven System unterrichten, für das Lehramtsstudium empfehlen, um eine adäquate Vorbereitung für inklusive Schulsysteme zu ermöglichen. Hierbei ging es sowohl um theoretische Inhalte und praktische Erfahrungen, als auch um die konkrete Umsetzung und Einbettung im Studium.

Alle Lehrkräfte sind sich einig darüber, dass das Lehramtsstudium eine Kombination aus theoretischen und praktischen Inhalten zum Themenspektrum Sonderpädagogik und inklusiver Unterricht umfassen muss, damit Lehrkräfte adäquat auf die Arbeit in inklusiven Schulsystemen vorbereitet werden können.

Theoretische und praktische Studieninhalte: Ein Teil der befragten Lehrkräfte beschreibt eine Art theoretischer Grundkenntnisse in der Sonderpädagogik mit folgenden Inhalten als nützlich: Techniken und Strategien in der Sonderpädagogik; Überblick, welche Strategien funktionieren und welche nicht; Behinderungen, Beeinträchtigungen und spezifische Bedürfnisse und deren Spektrum kennen und verstehen lernen.

Neben einführenden Kenntnissen in der Sonderpädagogik werden spezifische, pädagogische Fähigkeiten als notwendig erachtet: Zeit- und Verhaltensmanagement, grundlegende Psychologie, Aggressionsmanagement, aber auch die Fähigkeit, sich selbst und seine Tätigkeit einschätzen und reflektieren zu können und sich selbst zu schützen, um gesund zu bleiben.

Ergänzend zu theoretischen, einführenden Einheiten werden Einheiten bestehend aus praktischen Übungen als besonders hilfreich und lehrreich erachtet.

Während der Gespräche mit den Lehrkräften zeichnet sich eine Fähigkeit als besonders wichtig für inklusiven Unterricht heraus: das Differenzieren des Lehrplans, um individuelles und den Bedürfnissen jeden Kindes angepasstes Lernen zu ermöglichen:

„Special education units need to also have not only the understanding of the wide range of disabilities that students might have that come into schools but they also need to understand and to have knowledge of how to plan and change teaching practice to meet the needs."

„Learning how to differentiate the curriculum to create personal learning plans for every single child in the class room is terribly, terribly important. If we are genuinely about creating an includable society, then we need to be able to cater to the differences and reality of every child."

Voraussetzung hierfür ist es, Individualität zu verstehen und sein Augenmerk darauf zu legen, was ein Kind kann und nicht darauf, was es nicht kann:
„And else they need to know the whole motion that the impact disability has, and the importance of anyone who has any form of disability, that the teacher or other person focus on what the person can do not on what a person can't do. We focus on the process very much on what a person can't do and now an inclusion is all about what you can do."

Erst mit diesen Fähigkeiten können Studierende lernen, welche Methoden und Strategien es gibt, Lehrpläne zu differenzieren und den individuellen Bedürfnissen der Kinder anzupassen. Hierzu muss erlernt werden, wie man erkennt, wo ein Kind steht und was es braucht. Man muss die Lebenswelt und Lebensrealität des Kindes begreifen und überlegen, wie man Unterricht für das Kind interessant gestalten kann.

Drei Lehrkräfte weisen darauf hin, dass Theorien und Methoden auf bestimmten Gebieten hilfreich sein könnten, um sich auf spezielle Bedürfnisse ausrichten zu können:„There needs be theory, I think there needs be a push away from the generic lecture at university there needs to be getting more specialists in to talk about those specific areas rather than someone who uses a work book thinks I can teach all about these. There needs to be people who are specifically trained and have experience in a specific field to provide everyone with those strategies."

Zwei Lehrkräfte betonen außerdem, dass das Verständnis für die politischen Forderungen sehr wichtig ist, um inklusive Systeme und ihren Sinn zu verstehen: „At its base students need to a have a good understanding of concepts of discrimination (…). And that includes universities, colleges, training institutions and schools, so anyone is doing any form of education, needs to get some of those understandings 'cause it helps them understand what did this rights in terms of meeting the disability discrimination act.",,Definitely more policy, like looking at the different policies and making sure that those policies are includes in their programs and that they addressing the policies in their programs because I don't think that's happening. I think teachers are aware that there is, you know, the disability standards act but not much more is done with it. They try to althea to it, but they don't really know the document."

Aus den Gesprächen mit den Lehrkräften entstehen also folgende Empfehlungen für den Inhalt des Lehramtsstudiums:
- Theoretische Kenntnisse in der Sonderpädagogik:
- Überblick über Behinderungen und Bedürfnisse und deren Spektrum
- Überblick über Strategien und Methoden
- Grundlegende pädagogische Fähigkeiten:
- Grundlegende Psychologie
- Verhaltensmanagement
- Zeitmanagement
- Aggressionsmanagement
- Methoden der Selbsteinschätzung und -reflexion
- Methoden des Selbstschutzes
- Praktische Übungen für inklusiven Unterricht:
- Differenzierung des Lehrplans
- Erstellen von individuellen Lehrplänen
- Adressierung der Bedürfnisse jedes Kindes
- Spezifische Kurse mit Spezialisten (z.B. Autismus, Down-Syndrom, etc.)
- Grundlegendes pädagogisches Verständnis für inklusiven Unterricht:
- Individualität jedes Kindes
- Ressourcen und Stärken in den Mittelpunkt stellen
- Politische Grundsätze für Inklusion

Für die konkrete Umsetzung und Einbettung der Inhalte in das Lehramtsstudium empfehlen die befragten Lehrkräfte eine Implementierung während des gesamten Studiums, sodass der Themenkreis in jedem Semester unterrichtet wird. Außerdem sollten die Themen Sonderpädagogik und inklusiver Unterricht nicht nur als eigenständige Module unterrichtet, sondern in jedes spezifische Fach integriert werden, sodass man z.B. im Sport-Seminar durch praktische Übungen lernt, wie man Kinder mit Behinderungen im Sportunterricht adressieren kann.

Einbettung von Praktika Alle befragten Lehrkräfte sind sich weiterhin einig darüber, dass die Einbettung von Praktika in das Lehramtsstudium unerlässlich für eine adäquate Vorbereitung für das Lehren an einer inklusiven Schule ist. Da die befragten Lehrkräfte ihre Abschlüsse an unterschiedlichen Hochschulen

erworben haben, ist keine einheitliche praktische Vorbereitung zu erkennen. Mehrere Lehrkräfte berichten jedoch von folgender Einbettung von Praktika in das Studium: Innerhalb der vier Jahre des Studiums wurden vier Praktika absolviert und zwar ein Praktikum von drei Wochen im ersten Jahr, zwei Praktika von jeweils zwei Wochen im zweiten Jahr, ein Praktikum von zwei Wochen und eines von sechs Wochen im dritten Jahr und ein Praktikum von 20 Wochen am Ende des Studiums. Ausgehend von dieser Information schlägt die Mehrheit der befragten Lehrkräfte einen größeren Umfang und eine längere Dauer der Praktika vor. Es wird deutlich, dass hauptsächlich ein Praktikum im Sinne von Hospitation gemeint ist, da immer wieder betont wird, dass viele Strategien von erfahrenen Lehrkräften, sowohl in inklusiven als auch in Regelschulen, erlernt werden können:
„Class room experience I think is really helpful and watching others educated that have been in the system for a long time. And you gain by their experience more than someone just telling you."

"But I think it is a good idea that they do spend some time within their practicum period in looking, working in special classes I think that's a very good thing to include so they can understand the way the teachers change the curriculum or they change the teaching methods that sort of stuff."

Auch hinsichtlich des Settings des Praktikums werden verschiedene Vorschläge gemacht: sowohl Praktika in inklusiven Settings als auch Praktika in Regelschulen werden als hilfreich erachtet, da es um die Heterogenität und Individualität von Schülerinnen und Schülern generell geht. Ein großer Teil der befragten Personen macht jedoch deutlich, dass auf jeden Fall ein Praktikum in einer inklusiven Klasse oder Schule absolviert werden sollte. Eine Lehrkraft schlägt vor, dass ebenso ein Praktikum in einer Förderklasse oder -schule denkbar ist und eine andere Person sagt aus, dass sich ein Teil jedes Praktikums auf Kinder mit sonderpädagogischem Förderbedarf beziehen sollte. Einige Aussagen implizieren, dass die Praktika innerhalb des Studiums in verschiedenen Schulen bzw. Klassen mit unterschiedlichen Schülerinnen und Schülern mit unterschiedlichen Bedürfnissen absolviert werden sollten, sodass man die Möglichkeit hat, die Bandbreite an Heterogenität kennen und verstehen zu lernen:

„And maybe, you know working in different settings where there are different needs, a term in one and a term in another maybe not just the same."

Es werden außerdem zwei weitere Vorschläge zur Einbettung des Praktikums in das Lehramtsstudium gemacht: zum einen eine Art praktisches Jahr, in dem die Studierenden z.B. drei Tage der Woche in einer Schule und zwei Tage an der Universität verbringen; zum anderen die Einbettung von Beginn des Studiums bis zum Ende durch eine bestimmte Anzahl an Stunden (z.B. zwei oder vier Semesterwochenstunden), in denen man an einer Schule hospitiert in Kombination mit anschließenden Gesprächen mit der jeweiligen Lehrkraft. Durch diese Art der

Integrierung von Praktika bzw. Hospitation kann den Studierenden die Möglichkeit gegeben werden, über einen längeren Prozess inklusiven Unterricht kennenzulernen, eigene Fähigkeiten zu entwickeln und verschiedene Methoden und Strategien zu erlernen und zu reflektieren.

Weiterbildungen nach dem Studium Während der Gespräche mit den Lehrkräften wird vermehrt deutlich, welchen Stellenwert Weiterbildungen während der Tätigkeit als Lehrkraft einnehmen können. Ein großer Teil der befragten Lehrkräfte hat aufgrund der nicht integrierten Ausbildung zum inklusiven Unterricht verschiedene Weiterbildungsmöglichkeiten im Themenkreis Sonderpädagogik und inklusiver Unterricht wahrgenommen. Es wird jedoch auch berichtet, dass an einer der Schulen, in denen Lehrkräfte zum Interview rekrutiert wurden, an einem Nachmittag in der Woche fakultative Weiterbildungsmaßnahmen zu diversen Themen für das gesamte Kollegium stattfinden. So kann nicht nur eine gewisse Aktualität der Standards an der Schule gewährleistet werden, sondern auch die Auseinandersetzung mit Themen, die während der eigentlichen Ausbildung zur Lehrkraft eventuell vernachlässigt wurden.

6.6 Diskussion

Die vorgestellte Forschung zeigt, dass der Großteil der befragten australischen Lehrkräfte, nämlich zehn von 14, durch ihr Lehramtsstudium nicht auf das Unterrichten in inklusiven Schulen vorbereitet wurde bzw. sich nicht vorbereitet hierauf gefühlt hat. Auch die Einbettung von einzelnen Einheiten zu Sonderpädagogik oder Inklusion konnte diese Aufgabe nicht leisten. Auffällig ist, dass sich die Lehrkräfte vorbereitet gefühlt haben, die die genannte Thematik in einem gesonderten Studium (Bachelor Sonderpädagogik, Master Inclusive Education) oder in einem hohen Maße im Regellehramtsstudium studieren konnten. Hierdurch wird deutlich, dass das reguläre Lehramtsstudium in Australien, das die befragten Personen durchlaufen haben, nicht adäquat auf die Tätigkeit in inklusiven Schulsystemen vorbereitet.

Auch wird durch die Studie deutlich, dass in Australien ein anderes Lehrerausbildungssystem besteht als in Deutschland: der Bachelor dauert in Australien in der Regel vier Jahre und qualifiziert die Absolventinnen und Absolventen zu einer ordentlichen Lehrtätigkeit. Außerdem besteht die Möglichkeit, nach einem Bachelor-Studium in einem lehramtsfremden Fach (Bachelor of Arts/Bachelor of Science) ein einjähriges Diplom (Graduate Diploma of Education) zu absolvieren, welches dann zur Lehrtätigkeit an Schulen befähigt. Im Gegensatz hierzu benötigt man in Deutschland neben dem Bachelor, welcher in der Regel drei Jahre dauert, einen Master und weiterhin das Referendariat von (in den meisten Bundesländern derzeit noch) 1 ½ Jahren, bis man als vollständig ausgebildete

Lehrkraft an Schulen unterrichten darf. Deutsche Lehramtsanwärterinnen und -anwärter haben also im Vergleich zum australischen Ausbildungssystem eine längere Ausbildungsdauer. Dennoch zeigen diverse Studien und Fachliteratur, dass das Ausbildungssystem für Lehrkräfte in Deutschland die Thematik Sonderpädagogik und Inklusion nicht in einem solchen Umfang im Regellehramtsstudium integriert, als dass man von einer Vorbereitung auf die Tätigkeit in einem inklusiven Schulsystem sprechen könnte.

Die Befragung der australischen Lehrkräfte bestätigt die fachlich festgestellte Notwendigkeit der Umstrukturierung des Lehramtsstudiums durch die Einbettung von sonderpädagogischen und inklusiven Schwerpunkten. Die aufgezeigten vielseitigen Kompetenzen und die pädagogische Grundhaltung, über die eine Lehrkraft im inklusiven Schulsystem verfügen muss, können nur durch eine Vorbereitung im Studium erworben werden, die sowohl theoretische als auch praktische Kenntnisse im Umgang mit heterogenen Lerngruppen vermittelt.
Wenn die Zukunft des Bildungssystems in Deutschland die inklusive Schule ist – und dies muss die Zukunft sein, wenn die Bundesrepublik Deutschland den Anforderungen der UN-Konvention über die Rechte der Menschen mit Behinderung gerecht werden will – dann müssen auch die Lehrkräfte, die in diesem System arbeiten und es tragen, inklusive Lehrkräfte sein, die eine adäquate und professionelle Vorbereitung während ihres Studiums durchlaufen haben.

Transfer: Welche Veränderungen im Aufbau des Lehramtsstudiums in Deutschland sind notwendig

Der vorliegende Beitrag hat zusammenfassend dargestellt, dass eine Umstrukturierung des Lehramtsstudiums in Deutschland notwendig ist, um angehende Lehrkräfte auf inklusive Schulsysteme vorzubereiten. Die Tatsache, dass sich die in diesem Forschungsprojekt befragten australischen Lehrkräfte in der Mehrheit nicht auf die Lehrtätigkeit in inklusiven Klassen vorbereitet gefühlt haben, unterstützt die These, dass Lehramtsstudiengänge darauf ausgerichtet werden müssen, sonderpädagogische und inklusive Themen zu bearbeiten. Die Lehrkräfte haben betont, dass eine sowohl theoretische wie auch praktische Vorbereitung auf inklusive Settings während des Lehramtsstudiums unabdingbar sind, wenn Lehrkräfte den Anforderungen der heterogenen Lerngruppe gerecht werden sollen. Die Ergebnisse, die in Armidale, Australien erzielt wurden, können auf das Lehrerausbildungssystem übertragen werden, da die Anforderungen der inklusiven Schule weltweit dieselben sind.

Neben kurzfristigen Lösungsvorschlägen wie professionellen Fort- und Weiterbildungen für bereits tätige Lehrkräfte, gibt es verschiedene Vorschläge für langfristige Maßnahmen. Moser und Demmer-Dieckmann unterschieden vier momentan bestehende Lehrerausbildungsmodelle: 1. nebeneinander laufende Regellehramts- und Sonderpädagogiklehramtsstudiengänge, die kooperative Seminare zu einzelnen Schwerpunkten anbieten; 2. allgemeine Lehramtsstudiengänge, die sonderpädagogische Studieninhalte integrieren; 3. grundständige Lehramtsstudiengänge „Inklusive Pädagogik", die eine Doppelqualifizierung anbieten und 4. Masterstudiengänge, die aufbauend auf ein allgemeines Bachelor-Lehramtsstudium Zusatzqualifikationen bieten (Moser/ Demmer-Dieckmann 2013, S. 161f.).

Eine Beibehaltung der strukturellen Trennung der Lehramtsstudiengänge in allgemeines Lehramt und Sonderpädagogik-Lehramt kann den Anforderungen der UN-Konvention über die Rechte der Menschen mit Behinderung nicht im Ansatz gerecht werden und verliert bei der langfristigen Umstellung auf ein inklusives Bildungssystem in Deutschland seine Legitimation. Modell eins und zwei erweisen sich somit als nicht geeignet für die Ausbildungszukunft von Lehrkräften im inklusiven Schulsystem. Das dritte Modell kommt den Anforderungen der UN-Konvention zwar nahe (siehe z.b. Studiengang Inklusive Pädagogik an der Universität Bremen), dennoch stellt sich hier die Frage, wozu in inklusiven Bildungslandschaften Doppelqualifikationen auf lange Sicht notwendig sind und warum nicht stattdessen eine Qualifikation als inklusive Lehrkraft eingeführt wird. Hinzu kommt, dass diese Studiengänge (z.b. an der Universität Bremen) zwar darauf abzielen, eine Doppelqualifikation zu ermöglichen, vor dem Referendariat jedoch die Entscheidung getroffen werden muss, in welchem Berufsfeld man anschließend tätig sein will und dementsprechend den Vorbereitungsdienst absolviert. Dies entspricht dann weniger der Vorstellung einer inklusiven Schule für alle Lernenden. Gleiches gilt für das Angebot von inklusiven Lehramtsstudiengängen neben allgemeinen Lehramtsstudiengängen (siehe z.b. Studiengang „Kombi-Bachelor für das Lehramt an Grundschulen" und „Kombi-Bachelor für das Lehramt Grundschule mit Studienschwerpunkt integrierte Sonderpädagogik" an der Universität Bielefeld).

Heinrich et al. sehen perspektivisch ein stufenbezogenes, einheitlicheres Lehrerausbildungsmodell vor, das die verschiedenen Lehramtstypen aufhebt und schlagen folgende Ausbildungsziele vor: Lehramt inklusive Primarstufe, Lehramt Primarstufe mit Schwerpunkt Sonderpädagogik, Lehramt Sekundarstufe für allgemeine inklusive Schulen, Lehramt Sekundarstufe Schwerpunkt Sonderpädagogik und Master Schulbezogene Sonderpädagogik für Berufsfelder wie Beratung, Diagnostik und Förderzentren (Heinrich/ Urban/ Werning 2013, S. 109).

Ein grundständiger Lehramtsstudiengang für inklusive Schulsettings sollte neben dem fachlichen Wissen und den typischen Inhalten des allgemeinen Lehramtsstudiums folgende Inhalte transportieren:
- Grundlagen der Sozialpädagogik

- Grundlagen in den Entwicklungsbereichen Lernen, Sprache und emotional-soziale Entwicklung
- Grundlagen in den Entwicklungsbereichen Sehen, Hören, geistige und körperlich-motorische Entwicklung
- Grundlagen in den Bereichen Autismus, Down-Syndrom, etc.
- Kenntnisse im Bereich pädagogischer Diagnostik
- Didaktik und Methodik des Unterrichts in heterogenen Lerngruppen
- Kenntnisse im Bereich Organisationsentwicklung/Schulentwicklung
- Kenntnisse im Bereich Beratung
- Kenntnisse im Bereich Kommunikation und Klassenmanagement (Moser/ Demmer-Dieckmann 2013, S. 163).

Neben den theoretischen Inhalten des Studiums betont Amrhein die Bedeutung universitärer Praxisphasen (Amrhein 2011, S. 7ff.). Sie verweist damit auf das neue Schulgesetz in NRW, welches neben den integrierten Praktika ein Praxissemester vorschreibt. Sie plädiert für die Absolvierung des Praxissemesters in einem inklusiven Setting, sodass eine frühzeitige Professionalisierung für Inklusion angebahnt werden kann. Ebenso verweist sie darauf, dass eine universitäre Begleitung der Praxisphasen von großer Bedeutung für den Lernprozess der Studierenden ist und spricht sich somit für ein integriertes Seminar während der Praxisphasen aus (ebd., S. 9).

Erst die Verbindung von fachspezifischem Wissen, Inklusions- und sonderpädagogischem Wissen und den praktischen Erfahrungen in inklusiven Schulen und heterogenen Lerngruppen ermöglichen angehenden Lehrkräften eine adäquate Vorbereitung auf die Tätigkeit im inklusiven Schulsetting.

6.7 Literaturverzeichnis

Amrhein, B. (2011)- Inklusive LehrerInnenbildung – Chancen universitärer Praxisphasen nutzen. In: Zeitschrift für Inklusion, Ausgabe 3/2011. Online: (Stand: 09.02.2014)

European Agency (2012). Inklusionsorientierte Lehrerbildung. Ein Profil für inklusive Lehrerinnen und Lehrer. Online: http://schulentwicklung.uni-frankfurt.de/web/pdfs/Profile-of-Inclusive-Teachers-DE%20end.pdf (Stand: 09.02.2014)

Heinrich, M., Urban, M., Werning, R. (2013). Grundlagen, Handlungsstrategien und Forschungsperspektiven für die Ausbildung und Professionalisierung von Fachkräften für inklusive Schulen. In: Döbert, H., Weishaupt, H., (Hrsg.): Inklusive Bildung professionell gestalten. Situationsanalyse und Handlungsempfehlungen. Waxmann, Münster. S. 69-133.

Hillenbrand, C., Melzer, C., Hagen, T. (2013). Bildung schulischer Fachkräfte für inklusive Bildungssysteme. In: Döbert, H., Weishaupt, H., (Hrsg.): Inklusive Bildung professionell gestalten. Situationsanalyse und Handlungsempfehlungen. Waxmann, Münster. S. 33-68.

Hinz, A. (2012). Inklusion – historische Entwicklungslinien und internationale Kontexte. In: Hinz, A., Körner, I., Niehoff, U., (Hrsg.): Von der Integration zur Inklusion. Grundlagen – Perspektiven – Praxis. 3., durchgesehene Auflage, Lebenshilfe- Verlag, Marburg. S. 33-52.

Kultusministerkonferenz (2011). Inklusive Bildung von Kinder und Jugendlichen mit Behinderungen in Schulen. Beschluss der Kultusministerkonferenz vom 20.10.2011. Online: http://www.kmk.org/fileadmin/veroeffentlichungen_beschluesse/2011/2011_10_20-Inklusive-Bildung.pdf (Stand: 18.02.2014)

Mayring, P. (2010). Qualitative Inhaltsanalyse – Grundlagen und Techniken. 11. Auflage, Beltz Verlag, Weinheim und Basel.

Moser, V., Demmer-Dieckmann, I. (2013). Professionalisierung und Ausbildung von Lehrkräften für inklusive Schulen. In: Moser, V., (Hrsg.): Die inklusive Schule. Standards für die Umsetzung. Zweite Auflage, Verlag W. Kohlhammer, Stuttgart. S. 155-174.

Patt, R. (2012). Kommunale Strategien: Regionale Inklusionsplanung verbindlich gestalten. In: Reich, K., (Hrsg.): Inklusion und Bildungsgerechtigkeit. Standards und Regeln zur Umsetzung einer inklusiven Schule. Beltz Verlag, Weinheim und Basel. S. 205-219.

Reich, K. (2012). Inklusion und Bildungsgerechtigkeit – Standards und Regeln zur Umsetzung einer inklusiven Schule. Beltz Verlag, Weinheim und Basel.

Sawalies, J., Veber, M., Rott, D., Fischer, C., (2013). Inklusionspädagogik in der ersten Phase der Lehrerbildung. Eine explorative Studie zu Stand und Unterschieden universitärer Lehrangebote für die Regelschullehrämter. Zeitschrift Schulpädagogik heute, Lernen und Geschlecht, Heft 8 (2013). Prolog-Verlag. Online: http://www.google.de/url?sa=t&rct=j&q=&esrc=s&source=web&cd=1&ved=0CC4QFjAA&url=http%3A%2F%2Fwww.schulpaedagogik-heute.de%2Findex.php%2Fcomponent%2Fjoomdoc%2FSH_8%2FSH8_21b.pdf%2Fdownload&ei=R_IEU5jzOsuh7Aadv4CYAQ&usg=AFQjCNH1CA-q4ODM8UtT5aF-gtpU8FtPjOg&bvm=bv.61535280,d.ZGU (Stand: 19.02.2014)

Schlamp, K., Schlamp-Dieckmann, F. (2013). Praxisbuch Inklusion – Gemeinsames Lernen erfolgreich umsetzen. Verlag PRO Schule, Bonn.

Scholz, D. a (2012). Der Abschied vom Lernen im Gleichschritt. In: mittendrin e.V. (Hrsg.): Eine Schule für alle – Inklusion umsetzen in der Sekundarstufe. Verlag an der Ruhr, Mülheim an der Ruhr. S. 32-38.

Scholz, D. b (2012). Lehrer in neuen Rollen. In: : mittendrin e.V. (Hrsg.): Eine Schule für alle – Inklusion umsetzen in der Sekundarstufe. Verlag an der Ruhr, Mülheim an der Ruhr. S. 39-44.

Seitz, S., 2011: Eigentlich nichts Besonderes – Lehrkräfte für die inklusive Schule ausbilden. In: Zeitschrift für Inklusion, Ausgabe 3/2011. Online: http://www.inklusion-online.net/index.php/inklusion-online/article/view/83/83 (Stand: 10.02.2014)

Wocken, H. (2011). Was ist Inklusiver Unterricht? Eine Checkliste zur Zertifizierung schulischer Inklusion. In: Das Haus der inklusiven Schule. Baustellen – Baupläne – Bausteine. Feldhaus Verlag, Hamburg. S. 109- 139.

Katharina Steinbeck
7 Inclusive Schools - Inclusive Teachers? How much special needs preparation does a pre-service teacher need to teach successfully in an inclusive school system?

This chapter reports on a qualitative research project about the education of teachers at inclusive schools in Armidale, New South Wales (NSW) Australia.

7.1 Abstract

The ratification of the *UN Convention on the Rights of Persons with Disabilities* built the basis of the chance for an inclusive education system in Germany. Discussions amongst educational experts have concluded that teachers in Germany do not receive adequate preparation, concerning how to appropriately respond to the needs of special needs education and inclusive practices during their university studies, to fulfill the demands of an inclusive classroom. The reverse is true of most teachers in the NSW education system. The research project explores inclusive teacher practices in Australia, their tertiary preparation, and compares both Australian and German teacher preparation on what they can learn from each other. It is hoped that successful strategies can be transferred to the German system, highlighting that the training of effective inclusive teachers needs to include theoretical and practical experiences with diversity in classes and special needs education.
Keywords: teachers, inclusion, inclusive schools, special needs education, preparation, university studies

7.2 Inclusive Schools in Germany and Their Challenges

Since the ratification by Germany in 2009 of the *UN Convention on the Rights of Persons with Disabilities*, the country is obliged to facilitate the possibility of an equal and self-determined life for persons with disabilities. This includes the right to an education, as stated in Article 24 of the Convention. The difficulties the German education system has experienced implementing the Convention is evident in the German translation. For example, the English version of the original Convention text states:

"(…) States Parties shall ensure an inclusive education system at all levels and life long learning (…)", whereas the German translation states: "gewährleisten die Vertragsstaaten ein integratives Bildungssystem auf allen Ebenen und lebenslanges Lernen (…)" [Note the difference between inclusive and integrative, even though the German language also uses the word "inklusive".]

The German translation shows how strongly the tradition of the German education system is shaped by selection. An integrative educational landscape would mean that children with disabilities are to integrate into regular schools (Reich 2012 P.36). In contrast to this, inclusive schools would have to be equipped and able to accommodate and teach every pupil as an equal individual. The foundational success for this has to be implemented by the government (Reich 2012 p. 36). Hinz (2012) notes that the discussion of the relationship between 'integration' and 'inclusion' has been on-going since the year 2000 because the relationship is determined by the understanding of the terms themselves. By way of illustration, certain interpretations of the term 'integration' can also include a view of comprehensive integration in the sense that nobody is excluded (Hinz 2012 p. 40ff).

The first big challenge for the German education system is to re-structure the educational landscape from a *selective* to an *inclusive* system. Paragraph 2 of Article 24 of the *UN Convention on the Rights of Persons with Disabilities* states that: „persons with disabilities must not be excluded from the free of charge regular school system However, the School for Everybody is more than the formal opening of regular schools for students with disabilities through the means of additional special needs education in an otherwise unchanged school system" (Seitz 2011 p. 2).

Inclusion means to not only accept diversity, but to value it and recognise heterogeneity as a resource. Yet the basis for the successful implementation of inclusive practices in the education system would mean that society as a whole needs to adopt an inclusive view of people and the world. This pre-requisite is important as inclusion in the classroom cannot be successful if society keep living a discriminating and excluding norm. This means that successful inclusion needs to start with an essential mindset for without it, inclusion cannot succeed.

Another challenge for Germany implementing an inclusive education system was the ramifications of the Federal system reform held on the 1st September 2006. Central to this reform was the shifting of power and jurisdiction for education from the Federal to the State level (Patt 2012 p. 205). This shift in authority heralds significant differences regarding the progress and method concerning the introduction of inclusive schools (Schlamp/ Schlamp-Diekmann 2013, p. 18ff). One of the changes surrounds the geographical location of the student to their access of schools within their zone i.e. students can no longer choose any school they wish to attend. Equality in education can only be achieved when everybody has the same conditions and rights when accessing education, and should not be dependent upon their geographical location.

The change to an inclusive education system also begs the important question of which professionals take on which responsibilities. The implementation of Special Education teachers into regular schools with the responsibility of only teaching children with a diagnosed need for special education, does not serve the basic idea of inclusion justice. To illustrate, a regular school day would have students with special needs being taught by Special Needs teachers, and regular students being taught by regular teachers. It is undisputed that interdisciplinary cooperation is important, and there are many models of how regular education and special needs education can work together. However, to do the *UN Convention on the Rights of Persons with Disabilities* justice, all teacher education has to include inclusive education in its curriculum (Moser/ Demmer-Diekmann 2013, p. 155). Heinrich et al. also concludes that „a comprehensive special needs education of inclusion through individualisation is more in accordance with the basic idea of the *UN Convention on the Rights of Persons with Disabilities,* than a strict division of labour between the pedagogic task on one hand, and a psychological and/or medical-therapeutic task on the other hand" (Heinrich/ Urban/ Werning 2013, p. 78). Heinrich et al. (2013) therefore plead for the expansion of the knowledge of special needs education for regular and special needs education teachers (ibid., p.108).

7.3 The Challenges for Teachers at Inclusive Schools and their consequences

To make inclusive education possible the teachers are the most important element because they implement the inclusive system in the school. As a result, an inclusive school can only be as good as its teachers.

According to Wocken (2011), „inclusive education" means "that all children of an unselected and undivided group can access a general education to their individual ability and individual needs. In manifold learning processes with joint and differential learning situations; with utilisation of beneficial resources without impedient barriers to learning; and without discriminating and exclusionary practices, but with development-oriented evaluation of the learning process with active support of cooperating pedagogues and social networks." (Wocken 2011, p. 134).

How can teachers manifest Wocken's (2011) interpretation of inclusive education? To ensure inclusive teaching is successful, it is important for the teacher to internalise certain values and implement them accordingly. The *European*

Agency has compiled a profile of values inherent to successful inclusive teachers. One core value is the diversity of the students by viewing differences as resources, which suports the education of every student. Another value is that inclusive teachers support all students by promoting academic, emotional, social and practical learning, through an efficient teaching approach for heterogenic classes. A third value is the collaboration with parents, families and other educational professionals. The profile's last value for inclusive teachers is the acceptance of the fact that teaching is a learning activity, and teachers take responsibility for their lifelong learning. They should view their pre-service teacher education as a foundation for ongoing professional learning and development (European Agency 2012, p. 13ff.).

The shift to an inclusive education system also impacts upon the role of the teacher: in a regular class they are the main character, but in an inclusive classroom, they become more of an advisor or companion to the students (Scholz 2012, p. 39). Scholz notes that the shift to an inclusive classroom brings new challenges, chances and possibilities for both teacher and student, as the teacher's level of responsibility lessens, and the student's take more responsibility for their education. This may lead to a new lesson structure in which the teacher is responsible for giving the students an adequate learning environment and structuring it. Alongside the general framework the teacher provides, students can, and are to be involved in the planning and execution of lessons. Scholz states that the key to successful inclusive practices means the teacher has to change their basic attitude when it comes to heterogeneity: they need to view and accept differences within the group of learners, as well as promote a culture of trust in which the teacher trusts "that every pupil wants to learn and autonomously come to sensible constructions" (ibid., p.42).

Seitz (2011) emphasises that inclusive education does not mean to plan a lesson for regular students and then try to integrate special needs students in that lesson plan, rather to plan an individualised lesson for the entire group of learners from their perspective (Seitz 2011, p. 2f.). Heterogeneity has to be seen as a resource which helps the learning process. Saliwales et al. (2013) found that effective teachers in inclusive schools possessed a number of characteristics/factors. They included i) to understand inclusion as a social endeavour; ii) enact the basic principles of individual support; iii) differentiate diagnostic competences; iv) have the competence to lead a classroom; v) to organise lessons and other school-based activities; and vi) practice counseling competences and teamworking skills (Sawalies et al 2013, p. 4f.).

The changed role of the teacher in an inclusive classroom and the new understanding of the learning process in heterogenic learning groups, has the consequence that the education of teachers also needs changing to meet the challenges of the new learning environment and structure. Teachers have to learn an understanding of inclusion and inclusive processes, as well as the competences needed to implement inclusive structures. Article 24, Paragraph 4 the *UN Convention on the Rights of Persons with Disabilities* echoest this sentiment:

"In order to help ensure the realization of this right, States Parties shall take appropriate measures to employ teachers, including teachers with disabilities, who are qualified in sign language and/or Braille, and to train professionals and staff who work at all levels of education. Such training shall incorporate disability awareness and the use of appropriate augmentative and alternative modes, means and formats of communication, educational techniques and materials to support persons with disabilities."

The *Conference of Culture Ministers* in 2011 stated that in preparation for an inclusive system in Germany, the States are to provide basic and continued advanced education for teachers of all school forms (cf. Kultusministerkonferenz 2011, p. 20). This directive illustrates one of the consequences the State to Federal system shift had for the education system in Germany: the task for the States is officially stated, however, which method is employed is decided by every State. This can lead to big differences between the initiatives for the professionalisation of teachers for inclusive schools in different States (Hillenbrand et. Al. 2013, p. 37ff.).

To determine which competences pre-service teachers should learn to successfully promote inclusive practices, it may be useful to observe teachers who already work in such systems. For the past 10 years, schools in New South Wales, Australia operate within an inclusive education environment. This chapter reports on a research project involving discussions with Australian Primary school teachers about how effective their pre-service preparation was for preparing them to teach an inclusive classroom.

7.4 The Research Project: Teachers at Inclusive Schools in Armidale, Australia Research question

The idea for this research project came from conversations among German student teachers where the term "inclusion" created a general unease. According to our own statements, this unease is due to a lack of preparation for inclusive school systems during the teacher education. Yet how can an inclusive school system work when the teachers who are supposed to promote it are not prepared properly? The research question thereby evolved around the amount of special needs education required by pre-service teachers to adequately prepare them to teach effectively in inclusive school systems.

Data Collection and analysis
The interviews were held at two primary schools in Armidale over a period of two weeks. The schools were contacted by our co-operation partner in Armidale, the University of New England (UNE), New South Wales). A total of 14 teachers took part in an individual quantitative interview. At the first school, six interviews were held, all with female teachers. The other eight interviews were held at the second school; six with female and two with male teachers. The ratio between female and male participants was consistent with the ratio of female to male teachers at the schools. The selection of participants was random: teachers who had "free time" were invited to participate, and all teachers at both schools did.
The interviews averaged 10 minutes in length, were digitally recorded and fully transcribed for analysis and evaluation with the qualitative content analysis of Mayring (Mayring 2010, p. 68f.).

7.5 Results of the Research Project

Teacher Education and Preparation for an Inclusive School system
The 14 teachers interviewed in Armidale presented with a range of different tertiary qualifications as the table below reflects:

Number of teachers	Tertairy degree
6	Bachelor of Education (4 year degree)
3	Bachelor of Education (Primary) (3 year)
1	Bachelor of Education (Primary) (3 year) Master in Inclusive Education
1	Bachelor of Education (Primary) (3 year) Bachelor of Special Needs Education
1	Bachelor of Education (Primary) (3 year) Master of Teaching
2	Bachelor of Arts Master of Teaching
1 Teacher Aide	Bachelor of Nursing

Tabelle 7-1

Of 14 interviewed teachers,

No. of teachers	Classes studied at university	No. of Teachers and classes	Where SpEd info taught
9	Special Education/Inclusion	4 = Special needs education unit which	2 = Bachelor of Special Education

		went over one semester or year	1 = Master of Inclusive Education
		3 = The classes were conveying more theoretical and general information and were not very helpful. 1 = The special needs education unit was very helpful	
3	None		
2	Three or four units of special needs education	1 = Taught more general information 1 = Special needs education and inclusion were integrated to every class	
3			
1	Bachelor of Education (Primary) (3 year) Master of Teaching		
2	Bachelor of Arts Master of Teaching		

Tabelle 7-2

For example, during physical education class they were taught how to hold a physical education class in a way that children with disability can also be involved. It has to be noted that this teacher just finished her education, which leads to the conclusion that Australian universities are embedding special needs education and inclusive practice education more into their curriculum.

The teacher that had attained a *Master of Inclusive Education* spoke of the important insights this degree provided her:

„I completed a unit that focussed on Inclusive programming and developing Individual Education Plans (IEP's) with students. We looked at a range of needs ranging from high frequency disabilities and children with high support disabilities, right through to children on the lower end of the spectrum. The unit looked at different types of disabilities, policies that focused on injury, and a big focus was which program best met their needs".

Furthermore, the teachers were asked if they felt prepared for working with children with special needs/disabilities when they started their teaching position at the inclusive school. Only four of the 14 said they felt adequately prepared, whilst the remaining 10 said they did not feel prepared. Two of those ten said that they had hands-on training in an inclusive or special needs class, which made them feel more confident. Importantly, the four teachers who felt prepared were those who studied Special Needs education separately, or engaged in a lot of practical experience during their studies. Based on these findings, it would seem that a combination of regular teacher education and studying special needs education provides a healthy balance for teacher preparation at inclusive schools.

Suggestions for structuring teacher education
The focus of the research project was to identify which tertiary curriculum content, and how much tertiary content best prepared teachers who currently work in inclusive schools. The use of the term ‚curriculum content' incorporates tertiary theoretical information and practical experiences, as well as the actual implementation into their classrooms.

All teachers concured that in order to best prepare teachers for inclusive practices, a combination of theoretical content and practical context on special needs education and inclusive education is required.

Theoretical and practical curriculum contents
A number of teachers stated that a basic knowledge with the following information was especially helpful for them in their current role: A knowledge of techniques and strategies in Special Needs education; An overview of which strategies work and which don't; and An ability to identify and understand the range of learning disabilities, impairments and special need requirements across the Autistic spectrum. Teachers also identified that having the knowledge and ability to execute specific pedagogic skills were seen as highly important. These skills included: time management, behaviour management, an understanding of basic psychology, and the confidence and ability to manage aggression. The ability to assess and reflect upon oneself and one's actions was also considered a significant factor to staying healthy and avoiding burn-out.
The teachers viewed the blocks of Practicum in schools as especially helpful and informative. It was this first hand experience in classrooms that drew theory and practice together. All teachers agreed that central to the success of inclusive education was the teacher's ability to:

- „differentiate the curriculum to create personal learning plans for every single child in the class room";

- "understand the wide range of disabilities that students might have that come into schools, but they also need to understand and have the knowledge of how
- to plan and change teaching practice to meet these needs";
- "Learn how to differentiate the curriculum to create personal learning plans or every single child in the classroom";
- „Be able to cater to the differences and reality of every child".

One teacher claimed that a condition to achieving successful classroom differentiation is to understand individuality and to turn one's attention to what a child *can do,* and not what they *cannot do*:„Teachers need to understand the impact a disability can have upon someone, and focus upon what the person can do, and not upon what the person can't do. Currently some teachers tend to focus on the process of what a person can't do, and they will need to adapt because the concept of inclusion is all about what you can do."

Teachers need to try and understand the world and reality the child lives in, and think about how they can make learning more engaging and interesting. Three teachers mentioned how certain theories and sstrategies can be helpful when assessing and managing students with special needs:

"There needs be an understanding of theory. I think there needs be a push away from the generic lecture at university, and they need to get more specialists in to talk about those specific areas, rather than someone who thinks they can teach all about these areas. There needs to be people who are specifically trained and have experience in a specific field to provide everyone with those strategies."

Two teachers also stressed that an understanding of the policy and legal requirements are necessary to understand the importance of inclusive systems:"At a basic level, teachers need to have a good understanding of the concepts of discrimination, and that includes universities, Colleges, Training institutions and schools. So anyone involved in the education sector needs to know this because it helps them understand how students' rights fit in terms of meeting the *Disability Discrimination Act* requirements";"Having knowledge of different policies is important. You also have to make sure that those policies are included in their tertiary programs and that they know how to apply the policies in their classrooms, because I don't think that's happening. I think teachers are aware that there is the *Disability Discrimination Act,* and they try to adhere to it, but I don't think they really know the document well enough to do this".

Teachers suggested that the following topics be included in the curriculum of teacher education:

Theoretical knowledge in Special Needs education	Political requirements for inclusion
Overview of disabilities, their needs, across the Autistic spectrum	Highlighting resources and strengths
Methods for self-protection	Understanding of the individuality of every child
Basic pedagogy skills	Basic pedagogical understanding of inclusive teaching
Overview of classroom management strategies and methods	Specific classes delivered by experts e.g. Autism, Down Syndrome, etc.
Basic psychology	How to effectively address the needs of every child
Behaviour management	How to develop individual lesson plans
Time management	How to differentiate lesson plan content
Managing aggression	Methods to assess and reflect upon oneself

Tabelle 7-3

To successfully implement all of this content into teacher education, the teachers recommended that the content needed to be embedded across the four year degree, so the topics form part of the units each trimester. They suggested that the topics of special needs education and inclusive education should be implemented into every unit, rather than taught as stand-alone units.

Embedding practicum periods

All interviewed teachers agreed that the practicum time at schools was vital to best prepare the teacher fort he reality of teaching. A number of the interviewed teachers were awarded their degrees from different universities, and at that time, there were no standardised benchmarks so some techers had training in some areas whilst others didn't. practice. Currently, the Bachelor of Education (Primary) has their practicum periods embedded into their tertiary year. Over the four years, four practicum periods are completed as outlined in the table 7-4:

	First trimester	Second trimester
First year	5 dispersed days in school	
Second year		20 days
Third year		30 days

Fourth year		50 days

Tabelle 7-4

Most teachers suggested there be longer practicum periods that would provide the student teacher with more experience in the classroom. It became apparent that many strategies were taught by experienced teachers through the modelling of inclusive practices:
"The classroom experience is really helpful, and by watching teachers that have been in the system for a long time you learn from their experience more than someone just telling you";"I think it is a good idea that they spend some time in schools working in special classes so they can understand the way the teachers adapt the curriculum, or use different teaching methods".

Many teachers said that undertaking practicum periods in either an inclusive setting, or in a remedial class, together in a regular school was helpful as student teachers could observe how heterogeneity is managed in the classroom. Two additional suggestions for embedding practicum periods into the teacher education were made. The first one involved a kind of practical year in which the student teachers shared their time between school and university e.g. for three days a week at a school and two days at university. The second suggestion involved the student teacher spending a certain amount of hours e.g. two or four, at the school from the beginning to the end of the teacher education degree. This way, the student teacher can sit in on classes at a school and engage in regular conversations with the teacher. The student teacher observes how teachers operate in the classroom, and are able to observe first-hand how inclusive practices are implemented in response to student needs.

Further education
All teachers emphasised the importance of ongoing education and professional development to the effective management of students in an inclusive classroom. As a number of teachers claimed they had no specific preparation during their teacher education on inclusive and special education, many of them chose to educate themselves further on these subjects. At one of the schools, the Principal had set aside one afternoon each week for the entire teaching staff to meet and discuss related topics to these areas. These meetings ensured that all staff had a collective understanding and approach to how inclusive practices were managed at the school. Discussion: What changes are necessary in the German Education System? This chapter has highlighted that a restructuring of teacher education preparation in Germany is necessary to prepare prospective teachers for inclusive school systems.

There are a number of short-term solutions to promote inclusive practices in German schools such as the ongoing professional development of practising

teachers by experts in the areas of special and inclusive education topics. A long-term measure proposed by Moser and Demmer-Dieckmann (2013) differentiate between four teacher education models that are currently operating in Germany:
1. Parallel-running of regular and special needs teacher education which have cooperative seminars for certain topics;
2. General teacher education that integrates special needs education topics;
3. Undergraduate studies of "Inclusive Education" which offer a double qualification; and
4. A Master level study which would provide additional qualifications after a general Bachelor degree (Moser and Demmer-Dieckmann 2013, p. 161f.).

Keeping the regular and inclusive teacher education structurally separated cannot honor the *UN Convention on the Rights of Persons with Disabilities*. This means that models one and two of Moser and Demmer-Dieckmann (2013) suggestions are not suited for the future. The third model comes close to the requirements of the UN Convention e.g. the Degree course of Inclusive Pedagogy at the University of Bremen, but still the question remains why in Germany, double qualifications are necessary for teachers to teach in an inclusive education system – why not introduce the one qualification for inclusive teachers? Additionally, the aim of the degree course at the University of Bremen is to give the option of a double qualification, but before the internship can start, the student teacher needs to decide in which system they want to work and enrol in the corresponding preparation courses. Similarly, the University of Bielefeld offers inclusive teacher education alongside regular teacher education e.g. the degree course "Combined Bachelor for Teaching Primary School" and "Combined Bachelor for Teaching Primary School with Focus on Integrated Special Needs Education". These choices detracts from the concept of „inclusive schools for everyone".

Amrhein (2011) emphasised the importance of practical phases next to theoretical contents of teacher education (Amrhein 2011, p. 7ff.). She refers to the new education laws in North Rhine-Westphalia, which mandates a practical semester. She campaigned for the practical semester to take place in an inclusive setting so the practice of inclusion could begin earlier rather than later. She also noted that the university supervision of the practical phases is important for the learning process of the student teachers, and argued for an integrated seminar during the practical phases (ibid., p. 9).
Prospectively, Heinrich et al. stipulate a year-based, standardised model for teacher education which replaces the system of many different types of teacher education. They suggest following educational options:
i) a teaching degree in an inclusive primary school;
ii) a teaching degree in a primary school with a focus on special needs education;
iii) a teaching degree in a secondary school for regular inclusive schools;

iv) a teaching degree at a secondary school with focus on special needs education; and
v) a master's degree in school-related special needs education for vocational fields such as counselling, diagnostic and support centers (Heinrich/ Urban/ Werning 2013, p. 109).
Moser & Demmer-Dieckmann (2013) suggest that the contents of an undergraduate teaching degree for inclusive school settings should include, alongside expert knowledge and the regular contents of regular teacher education, the following:

- basics of social pedagogy
- basics in the child development areas learning, language and social-emotional development
- basics in the child development areas seeing, hearing, mental and motor development
- basics in the areas autism, down syndrome, etc.
- knowledge in the area pedagogic diagnostics
- didactics and methods for teaching heterogenic learning groups
- knowledge in the areas organisational development/school development
- knowledge in the area of consulting
- knowledge in the areas of communication and class management (Moser and Demmer-Dieckmann 2013, p. 163).

7.6 Discussion

The project showed that 10 of the 14 teachers believed they were not adequately prepared in their tertiary training to teach effectively at inclusive schools, and currently did not feel confident in doing so. Despite ongoing education regarding special needs or inclusive education, teachers still lacked the professional and personal confidence to implement strateges in their classrooms. Noticeably, only the teachers who had studied special needs education or inclusive education separately, or studied these subjects during their teacher education preparation, felt confident to teach at an inclusive school. Therefore, these conclusions highlight the importance of preparing student teachers in the areas of special and inclusive education at the tertiary level.

The study also highlighted differences between the Australian and German teacher education systems. In Australia to attain a Bachelor's degree in Education, a student needs to study a four year degree to qualify as a teacher. Conversely in Germany, students need to complete a three year Education degree, and then complete a Master degree and spend 18 months at a school on an internship.

Hence, German student teachers have a longer teacher preparation time than Australian student teachers. Despite this, many studies and specialist literature report that the German teacher education system does not integrate the subjects of special needs and inclusive education into their teacher preparation.

The Australian teachers suggested that their tertairy teacher education preparation needs to be revisited to include more emphasis on special needs and inclusive education units. According to the teachers, the presented competences and pedagogic attitude outlined in this chapter, can only be achieved during teacher education preparation, where theoretical and practical knowledge comes together during practicum placements.

As the German education system prepares to honor the *UN Convention on the Rights of Persons with Disabilities* and embed the concept of inclusive education throughout their schools, then the teachers who work in and carry this system need to have the adequate and professional preparation during their teacher education.

Only the combination of specialised knowledge, knowledge about inclusion and special needs education, and the practical experience at inclusive schools with a heterogenic group of learners, will adequately prepare teachers for teaching in an inclusive school setting.

7.7 References

Amrhein, B. (2011)- Inklusive LehrerInnenbildung – Chancen universitärer Praxisphasen nutzen. In: Zeitschrift für Inklusion, Ausgabe 3/2011. Online: (Stand: 09.02.2014)

European Agency (2012). Inklusionsorientierte Lehrerbildung. Ein Profil für inklusive Lehrerinnen und Lehrer. Online: http://schulentwicklung.uni-frankfurt.de/web/pdfs/Profile-of-Inclusive-Teachers-DE%20end.pdf (Stand: 09.02.2014)

Heinrich, M., Urban, M., Werning, R. (2013). Grundlagen, Handlungsstrategien und Forschungsperspektiven für die Ausbildung und Professionalisierung von Fachkräften für inklusive Schulen. In: Döbert, H., Weishaupt, H., (Hrsg.): Inklusive Bildung professionell gestalten. Situationsanalyse und Handlungsempfehlungen. Waxmann, Münster. S. 69-133.

Hillenbrand, C., Melzer, C., Hagen, T. (2013). Bildung schulischer Fachkräfte für inklusive Bildungssysteme. In: Döbert, H., Weishaupt, H., (Hrsg.): Inklusive Bildung professionell gestalten. Situationsanalyse und Handlungsempfehlungen. Waxmann, Münster. S. 33-68.

Hinz, A. (2012). Inklusion – historische Entwicklungslinien und internationale Kontexte. In: Hinz, A., Körner, I., Niehoff, U., (Hrsg.): Von der Integration zur Inklusion. Grundlagen – Perspektiven – Praxis. 3., durchgesehene Auflage, Lebenshilfe- Verlag, Marburg. S. 33-52.

Kultusministerkonferenz (2011). Inklusive Bildung von Kinder und Jugendlichen mit Behinderungen in Schulen. Beschluss der Kultusministerkonferenz vom 20.10.2011. Online: http://www.kmk.org/fileadmin/veroeffentlichungen_beschluesse/2011/2011_10_20-Inklusive-Bildung.pdf (Stand: 18.02.2014)

Mayring, P. (2010). Qualitative Inhaltsanalyse – Grundlagen und Techniken. 11. Auflage, Beltz Verlag, Weinheim und Basel.

Moser, V., Demmer-Dieckmann, I. (2013). Professionalisierung und Ausbildung von Lehrkräften für inklusive Schulen. In: Moser, V., (Hrsg.): Die inklusive Schule. Standards für die Umsetzung. Zweite Auflage, Verlag W. Kohlhammer, Stuttgart. S. 155-174.

Patt, R. (2012). Kommunale Strategien: Regionale Inklusionsplanung verbindlich gestalten. In: Reich, K., (Hrsg.): Inklusion und Bildungsgerechtigkeit. Standards und Regeln zur Umsetzung einer inklusiven Schule. Beltz Verlag, Weinheim und Basel. S. 205-219.

Reich, K. (2012). Inklusion und Bildungsgerechtigkeit – Standards und Regeln zur Umsetzung einer inklusiven Schule. Beltz Verlag, Weinheim und Basel.

Sawalies, J., Veber, M., Rott, D., Fischer, C., (2013). Inklusionspädagogik in der ersten Phase der Lehrerbildung. Eine explorative Studie zu Stand und Unterschieden universitärer Lehrangebote für die Regelschullehrämter. Zeitschrift Schulpädagogik heute, Lernen und Geschlecht, Heft 8 (2013). Prolog-Verlag. Online: http://www.google.de/url?sa=t&rct=j&q=&esrc=s&source=web&cd=1&ved=0CC4QFjAA&url=http%3A%2F%2Fwww.schulpaedagogik-heute.de%2Findex.php%2Fcomponent%2Fjoomdoc%2FSH_8%2FSH8_21b.pdf%2Fdownload&ei=R_IEU5jzOsuh7Aadv4CYAQ&usg=AFQjCNH1CA-q4ODM8UtT5aF-gtpU8FtPjOg&bvm=bv.61535280,d.ZGU (Stand: 19.02.2014)

Schlamp, K., Schlamp-Diekmann, F. (2013). Praxisbuch Inklusion – Gemeinsames Lernen erfolgreich umsetzen. Verlag PRO Schule, Bonn.

Scholz, D. a (2012). Der Abschied vom Lernen im Gleichschritt. In: mittendrin e.V. (Hrsg.): Eine Schule für alle – Inklusion umsetzen in der Sekundarstufe. Verlag an der Ruhr, Mülheim an der Ruhr. S. 32-38.

Scholz, D. b (2012). Lehrer in neuen Rollen. In: : mittendrin e.V. (Hrsg.): Eine Schule für alle – Inklusion umsetzen in der Sekundarstufe. Verlag an der Ruhr, Mülheim an der Ruhr. S. 39-44.

Seitz, S., 2011: Eigentlich nichts Besonderes – Lehrkräfte für die inklusive Schule ausbilden. In: Zeitschrift für Inklusion, Ausgabe 3/2011. Online: http://www.inklusion-online.net/index.php/inklusion-online/article/view/83/83 (Stand: 10.02.2014)

Wocken, H. (2011). Was ist Inklusiver Unterricht? Eine Checkliste zur Zertifizierung schulischer Inklusion. In: Das Haus der inklusiven Schule. Baustellen – Baupläne – Bausteine. Feldhaus Verlag, Hamburg. S. 109-139.

The manufacturer's authorised representative in the EU is Springer Nature Customer Service Centre GmbH, Europaplatz 3, 69115 Heidelberg, Germany. If you have any concerns regarding our products, please contact ProductSafety@springernature.com

Printed and bound by CPI Group (UK) Ltd, Croydon, CR0 4YY

25/03/2026

02078214-0006